SCHOLASTIC
OAN

50

LITERACY HOURS FOR LESS ABLE LEARNERS

- Tricky topics covered
- Shared texts for a lower reading age
- Photocopiable activities

AGES
5-7

372.
6
FiF

Louise Carruthers

107   TES

CREDITS

Author
Louise Carruthers

Illustrations
Gaynor Berry

Editor
Victoria Lee

Series Designer
Anna Oliwa

Assistant Editor
Jane Gartside

Designer
Anna Oliwa

Text © Louise Carruthers
© 2005 Scholastic Ltd

Designed using Adobe® InDesign®

Published by Scholastic Ltd
Villiers House
Clarendon Avenue
Leamington Spa
Warwickshire CV32 5PR

www.scholastic.co.uk

Printed by Bell & Bain Ltd, Glasgow

3 4 5 6 7 8 9   6 7 8 9 0 1 2 3 4

UNIVERSITY OF CHICHESTER

ACKNOWLEDGEMENTS

The publishers gratefully acknowledge permission to reproduce the following
copyright material:
John Foster for 'Walking Round the Zoo' by John Foster from *Themes for Early Years: Myself* compiled by Irene Yates © 1995, John Foster (1995, Scholastic Limited).
Harcourt Education for extracts from *Animal Young: Birds* by Rod Theodorou © 2000, Rod Theodorou (2000, Heinemann Library). **David Higham Associates** for an extract from *The Minpins* by Roald Dahl © 1991, Roald Dahl (1991, Jonathan Cape Limited).
Hodder and Stoughton Limited for an extract from *Goldilocks and The Three Bears* by Penelope Lively © 1997, Penelope Lively (1997, Wayland). **Nord-Süd Verlag A G Gossau Zurich** for an extract and illustration from *Little Polar Bear* by Hans de Beer. First published in Switzerland by Nord-Süd Verlag A G Gossau Zurich, Switzerland under the title *Kleiner Eisbär, Wohin Fährst Du*. English text and illustration © 1987, Hans de Beer (1987, Nord-Süd). **The Orion Publishing Group Ltd** for an extract and an illustration 'Horrid Henry Gets Rich Quick' from "Horrid Henry's Nits" by Francesca Simon © 2001, Francesca Simon (2001, Orion Children's Books)and for the use of an extract from 'Father Bear and the Naughty Bear Cubs' from *How to Count Crocodiles*, by Margaret Mayo © 1994, Margaret Mayo (1994, Orion Children's Books).
The Random House Group for uses of an illustration by Patrick Benson from *The Minpins* by Roald Dahl ©1991, Patrick Benson (1991, Jonathan Cape Limited). **Scholastic Childrens Books** for extracts 'Humpty Dumpty Sat on the Wall' and 'Hey Diddle Diddle' from *Hairy Tales and Nursery Crimes* by Michael Rosen ©1985, Michael Rosen (1985, André Deutsch Limited). **The Scripture Union** for allowing the rewriting of a poem based on 'What are friends like?' by Ruth Kirtley from *Sing, Say and Move* compiled by Jill McWilliam © 1981, Scripture Union. **Charles Thomson** for 'People in the house' by Charles Thomson from *Scholastic Collections: Early Years Poems and Rhymes* complied by Jill Bennett © 1993, Charles Thomson (1993, Scholastic Ltd). **Usborne Publishing Ltd** for an extract from *Beginners: Tadpoles and Frogs* by Anna Milbourne © 2002, Usborne Publishing Ltd (2002, Usborne Publishing Ltd).

British Library Cataloguing-in-Publication Data
A catalogue record for this book is available from the British Library.

ISBN-10 0-439-97177-2
ISBN-13 978-0439-97177-5

The right of Louise Carruthers to be identified as the author of this work has been asserted by her in accordance with the Copyright, Designs and Patents Act 1988.

Extracts from *The National Literacy Strategy* © Crown copyright. Reproduced under the terms of HMSO Guidance Note 8.

372.

6

FIF

Contents

50 LITERACY HOURS
FOR LESS ABLE LEARNERS AGES 5 TO 7

This series of three books provides a range of activities with the less able learners in any classroom in mind. The activities cover many of the main objectives in *The National Literacy Strategy* (NLS) at word, sentence and text level.

Each lesson uses photocopiable games, activities and examples designed to help the slower learner understand and develop and expand their literacy when reading, writing, speaking and listening. The lesson plans are designed to:

● enable teachers to explain word- and sentence-level work in a simple, step-by-step approach

● guide the writing process by giving the teacher suggestions to model and ideas for sharing and planning in relation to text-level work

● motivate the children with engaging activities and games

● address different learning styles and levels by providing a variety of activities.

About the book

Each book is made up of 50 lesson plans with an accompanying photocopiable activity and, in order to make the book simple to use, the lessons all follow a similar pattern. At the back of the book are photocopiable text extracts that can be used to address the text-level criteria, providing the teacher with good examples from children's literature as and when it is needed.

How to use this book

Each lesson is written to address one or two specific NLS objectives from Years 1 and 2 and these are given at the start of each lesson plan. The objectives grid at the beginning of the book shows tracking back, if the subject area has already been introduced in Reception.

These lessons will help you to teach literacy in a creative and inspiring way. The activities are designed for practising and reinforcing learning from the beginning part of the lesson. The independent activities, usually produced as photocopiable sheets, are presented in a variety of formats to try to accommodate a range of learning styles, and the children should be encouraged to work with as little adult support as possible.

The Plenary may be a brief assessment and review, a few more turns of a game or a quick variation on the main activity. The lessons and accompanying photocopiable activities in the book are written as stand-alone units and can be used by the teacher or teaching assistant at any point in the school year. The activities are designed to fit into the individual teacher's planning for literacy.

Title of Lesson	Y2 Objective/s	Y1 Objective/s or Tracking Back	YR
High frequency words		**T1. W9:** Read on sight high frequency words identified for Y1/Y2 from Appendix List 1. **T1. S4:** Write captions and simple sentences, and to re-read, recognising whether or not they make sense, for example: missing words, wrong word order.	W6.
Rhyming strings		**T1. W1:** To generate rhyming strings. **T1. W5:** To blend phonemes to read CVC words in rhyming and non-rhyming sets.	W1. W4.
Consonant clusters		**T2. W3:** To discriminate, read and spell words with initial consonant clusters - Appendix List 3.	
Long vowel phonemes	**T2. W1:** To secure the reading and spelling of words containing different spellings of the long vowel phonemes from Year 1.	**T3. W1:** To learn the common spelling patterns for each of the long vowel phonemes.	
Sentences	**T2. S9:** To secure the use of simple sentences in own writing.	**T2. S6:** To use the term *sentence* appropriately to identify sentences in text.	
Capital letters and full stops		**T2. S5:** To continue demarcating sentences in writing, ending a sentence with a full stop. **T2. S7:** To use capital letters for the personal pronoun *I*, for names and the start of a sentence.	S1.
Word order		**T3. S4:** To learn about word order. **T3. S6:** To reinforce knowledge of the term *sentence*.	S1. S3.
Missing words		**T1-3. S2:** To use awareness of the grammar of a sentence to decipher new or unfamiliar words. **T2. S3:** To predict words from preceding words in sentences and investigate the sorts of words that 'fit', suggesting appropriate alternatives.	W1. W2.
Asking or telling		**T3. S7:** To add question marks to questions. **T3. T19:** To identify simple questions.	
Asking questions	**T3. S6:** To learn a range of '*wh*' words typically used to open questions: *what, where, when, who* and to add question marks.	**T3. S7:** To add question marks to questions.	
Speech bubbles	**T2. S2:** To read aloud with intonation and expression appropriate to the grammar and punctuation. **T2. S7:** To recognise and use speech bubbles as an alternative way of presenting text.		
Exclamation marks	**T2. S2:** To read aloud with intonation and expression appropriate to the grammar and punctuation (sentences, speech marks, exclamation marks). **T2. S9:** To secure the use of simple sentences in own writing.	**T1. S3:** To draw on grammatical awareness to read with appropriate expression and intonation. **T3. S6:** Through reading and writing, to reinforce knowledge of term sentence from previous terms.	
Connectives	**T1. S2:** To find examples, in fiction and non fiction, of words and phrases which link sentences. **T2. S9:** To secure the use of simple sentences in own writing.	**T2. S5:** To continue demarcating sentences in writing, ending a sentence with a full stop.	
Natalie Noun	**T1. W10:** To build individual collections of personal interest or significant words.	**T3. W8:** To make collections of personal interest or significant words.	
Annie Adjective	**T1. W5:** To read on sight and spell approximately 30 more words from Appendix List 1.	**T2. S5:** To continue demarcating sentences in writing, ending a sentence with a full stop. **T2. S7:** To use capital letters for the personal pronoun I, for names and for the start of a sentence.	
Synonyms	**T3. W10:** To use synonyms and other alternative words/phrases that express same or similar meanings; to collect, discuss similarities and shades of meaning and use to extend and enhance writing.	**T3. W8:** To make collections of personal interest or significant words and words linked to particular topics.	
Proper nouns	**T1. W5:** To read on sight and spell approximately 30 more words from Appendix List 1.	**T3. S5:** To learn other common uses of capitalisation. **T2. W6:** To read on sight approx. 30 more words from Appendix List 1.	S4.
Vernon Verb	**T2. S5:** To use verb tenses with increasing accuracy in speaking and writing, eg catch/caught, see/saw.	**T2. S5:** To continue demarcating sentences in writing , ending a sentence with a full stop.	
Adding -*ing*	**T2. S4:** Be aware of need for gramSmatical agreement in speech/writing, match verbs to nouns/pronouns correctly.	**T3. W6:** To investigate and learn spellings of verbs with '*ing*' (present tense) endings.	T1. W7.
Adding -*ed*	**T1. W7:** To use word ending '*ed*' (past) to support their reading and spelling. **T2. S5:** To use verb tenses with increas-ing accuracy in speaking and writing.	**T3. W6:** To investigate and learn spellings of verbs with '*ed*' (past tense) endings.	
Plurals		**T2. W8:** To investigate and learn spellings of words with 's' for plurals.	

NLS OBJECTIVES

Title of Lesson	Y2 Objective/s	Y1 Objective/s or Tracking Back	YR
Syllables	**T2. W5:** To discriminate, orally, syllables in multi-syllabic words using children's names and words from their reading.		
Compound words	**T2. W4:** To split familiar oral/written com- pound words into their component parts.		
Vowels and consonants		**T1. W4:** To discriminate and segment all three phonemes in CVC words. **T3. W9:** To use the terms 'vowel' and 'consonant'.	W2. W3.
Alphabetical order		**T1. W2:** To practise alphabetic letter knowledge and alphabetic order.	W2. W3.
Predictable and repeating patterns		**T1. T6:** To recite stories and rhymes with predictable and repeating patterns. **T1. T10:** To use rhymes and patterned stories as models for their writing.	T10. T14.
Traditional tale		**T1-3. T2:** To use phonological, contextual, grammatical and graphic knowledge to work out, predict and check the meanings of unfamiliar words and to make sense of what they read. **T3. T5:** To re-tell stories, to give the main points in sequence and to pick out significant incidents.	T7. T8.
Story box	**T1. T5:** To identify and discuss reasons for events in stories linked to plot. **T2. T4:** To predict story endings/incidents while reading with the teacher.	**T2. T7:** To discuss reasons for, or causes of, incidents in stories.	T9.
Story opening		**T1. T5:** To describe story settings and incidents and relate them to own experience and that of others. **T2. T14:** To represent outlines of story plots using, eg captions, pictures, arrows to record main incidents in order.	T12.
Character and dialogue		**T2. T9:** To become aware of character and dialogue. **T3. S3:** To read familiar texts aloud with pace and expression appropriate to the grammar. **T3. S5:** Other common uses of capitalisation, for example: for emphasis.	
Characters		**T2. T8:** To identify and discuss characters, eg appearance, behaviour, qualities; to speculate about how they might behave; to discuss how they are described in the text; and to compare characters from different stories or plays. **T2. T15:** To build simple profiles of characters from stories read, describing characteristics, appearance, behaviour with pictures, single words, captions, words and sentences from text.	
Character profile	**T2. T6:** To identify and describe characters, expressing own views and using words/phrases from the text. **T2. T14:** To write character profiles, for example: simple descriptions, using key words and phrases spoken by characters in text.	**T2. T8:** To identify and discuss characters, eg appearance, behaviour, qualities; to speculate about how they might behave; to discuss how they are described in the text; and to compare characters from different stories or plays.	
Story writing		**T1. T9:** Write about events in personal experience linked to a variety of familiar incidents from stories. **T1-3. T2:** To use phonological, contextual, grammatical and graphic knowledge to work out, predict and check the meanings of unfamiliar words and to make sense of what they read. **T2. T7:** To discuss reasons for causes of incidents in stories.	
Setting	**T2. T5:** To discuss story settings, to compare differences, to locate key words and phrases in text, to consider how different settings influence events and behaviour. **T2. T13:** To use story settings from reading.		
Rhyming poetry		**T1. T6:** To recite stories and rhymes with predictable and repeating patterns, extemporising on patterns orally by substituting words and phrases, extending patterns, inventing patterns and playing with rhymes. **T1. T10:** To use rhymes and patterned stories as models for their own writing.	W1. T10.
Nursery rhymes		**T1. T4:** To read familiar simple stories and poems independently, to point while reading and make correspondence between words said and read. **T1. T10:** To use rhymed and patterned stories as models for their own writing.	S3. T1.

Title of Lesson	Y2 Objective/s	Y1 Objective/s or Tracking Back	YR
Action rhymes		**T2. T11:** To learn and recite simple poems and rhymes, with actions, and to re-read them from the text. **T2. T13:** To substitute and extend patterns from reading through language play, eg by using same lines and adding new words.	T14.
Friendship poems		**T1–3. S2:** To use awareness of the grammar of a sentence to decipher new or unfamiliar words. **T3. T9:** To read a variety of poems on similar themes. **T3. T15:** To use poems or parts of poems as models for own writing.	T1. T7. T2. T9.
Alliteration	**T1. T7:** To learn, re-read and recite favourite poems, taking account of punctuation; to comment on aspects such as word combinations, sound patterns and forms of presentation. **T1.T12:** Use simple poetry structures, substitute own ideas, write new lines.	**T2. T13:** To substitute and extend patterns from reading through language play, eg by extending alliterative patterns.	T14.
Fiction and non-fiction		**T2. T17:** To use terms 'fiction' and 'non-fiction', noting some of their differing features, eg layout, titles, contents page, use of pictures, labelled diagrams.	
Contents page		**T2. T18:** To read non-fiction books and understand that the reader doesn't need to go from start to finish but selects according to what is needed. **T2. T21:** To understand the purpose of contents pages and indexes and to begin to locate information by page numbers and words by initial letter.	
Non-chronological reports		**T2. T17:** To use terms 'fiction' and 'non-fiction', noting some of their differing features. **T2. T25:** To use simple sentences to describe, based on examples from reading; to write simple non-chronological reports.	
Explanation	**T1–3. T2:** To use phonological, contextual, grammatical and graphic knowledge to work out, predict and check the meanings of unfamiliar words and to make sense of what they read. **T2. T19:** To read flow charts and cyclical diagrams that explain a process. **T2. T21:** To produce simple flow charts or diagrams that explain a process.	**T2. T22:** To write labels for drawings and diagrams.	T12.
Captions		**T1. S8:** To begin using full stops to demarcate sentences. **T1. T14:** To write simple captions.	T11. T12. T13.
Labels		**T2. T22** To write labels for drawings and diagrams.	T11. T12.
Instructions 1	**T1. T13:** To read simple written instructions. **T1. T14:** To note key structural features. **T1. T16:** To use models from reading to organise instructions sequentially.	**T1. T13** To read and follow simple instructions.	T1.
Instructions 2	**T1. T13:** To read simple written instructions. **T1. T15:** To write simple instructions. **T1. T18:** To use appropriate register in writing instructions.	**T1. T13** To read and follow simple instructions.	T1.
Writing a list		**T1. T15** To make simple lists for planning, reminding etc	T11. T15.
Recount	**T1. T11:** To use language of time to structure a sequence of events, for example: when I had finished, suddenly, after that.	**T3. T18** To read recounts and begin to recognise generic structure, eg ordered sequence of events, use of words like first, next, after, when.	
Dictionary work	**T2. T16:** Use dictionaries and glossaries to locate words by using initial letter. **T2. T17:** To know that dictionaries and glossaries give definitions and explanations. **T2. T20:** Make class dictionaries and glossaries, giving explanations/definitions.	**T1. W2** To practise and secure alphabetic letter knowledge and alphabetic order.	W2. W3.

High frequency words

Objectives
Y1. T1. W9.
To read on sight approximately 30 high frequency words identified for Y1 and Y2 from Appendix List 1.

Y1. T1. S4.
To write captions and simple sentences, and to re-read, recognising whether or not they make sense, for example, missing words, wrong word order.

Guided work

1. Prepare a set of A4 cards of the words you have chosen to focus on, for example, from the sheet opposite: *I like to go to school.*

2. Give each child in the group a word card. Ask if any of the children can read their word. Encourage the children to try to sound the word out if appropriate. Tell the group words they cannot read.

3. Ask the children to stand up and arrange themselves so that the words make a sentence when read in order. Depending on the ability of the children, it may be necessary to tell them the sentence you want them to make. Ask what is missing from the end of the sentence (a full stop). Give the person holding the last word in the sentence a full stop to hold up to mark the end of the sentence.

4. Stick the word cards in order on a board or peg them on a washing line. Read the sentence with the children, emphasising one-to-one correspondence between the spoken and written word. Ask different children to stand up and read the sentence to the rest of the group.

5. Tell the children to close their eyes. Remove one of the words from the sentence. Ask the children to try to work out which word has disappeared. Repeat this activity, removing a different word from the sentence each time. Change the game by swapping two words over and asking the children to correct the word order. Then ask them to read the sentence.

Independent work

● Put the children in pairs to play the word game on the sheet opposite. Give each pair of children a copy of the gameboard, two counters and dice. Place a set of word cards for each player in the centre of the board. You may wish to adapt the gameboard and make different word cards according to the words you are teaching. Explain the rules of the game. Tell the children to take it in turns to roll the dice and move their counter the appropriate number of spaces around the board. If a child lands on a word, they must try to read it. If they read the word correctly, they may collect that word from the central pile and roll the dice again. If they are unable to read the word or land on a word they have already collected, play passes to the other player. Play continues until one child has collected a full stop and all of the words required to make the sentence. The winner shouts: 'Sentence!'

Plenary

● Conclude the session with some flash-card work to practise recognition of these and other high frequency words.

Further support
● Rather than introducing five or six new words in a session, you could use one new word in a sentence with which the children are familiar.
● As the children become confident, you could adapt the game to include a variety of words and ask the children to construct their own sentences.

Word game

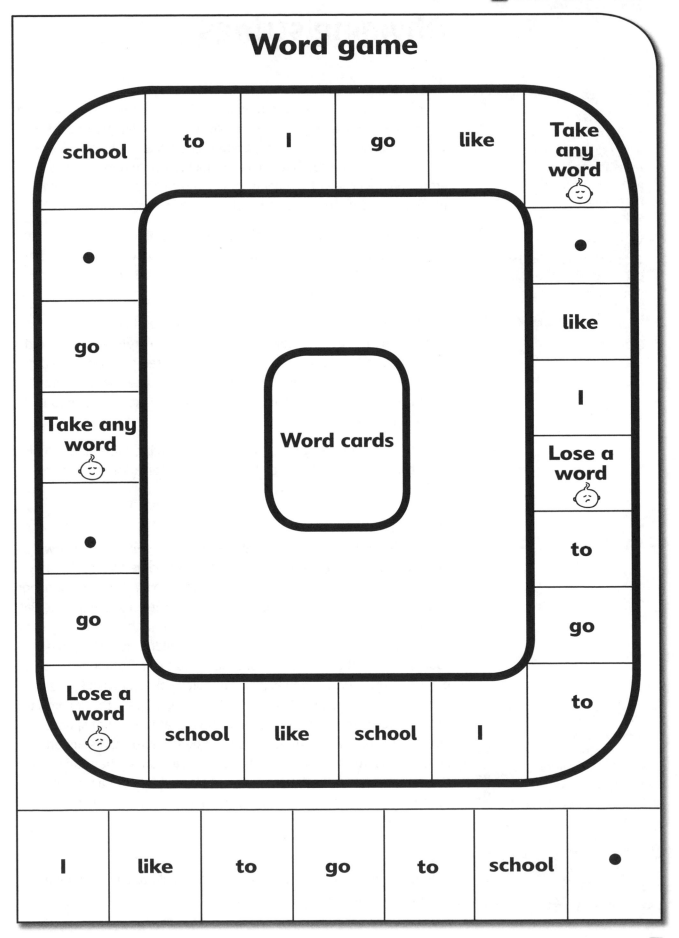

Rhyming strings

Objectives

Y1. T1. W1.
To practise and secure the ability to rhyme, and to relate this to spelling patterns through generating rhyming strings.

Y1. T1. W5.
To blend phonemes to read CVC words in rhyming and non-rhyming sets.

Guided work

1. This lesson focuses on the rhyming strings *at* and *og*. You will need a toy cat and dog or, if you have not got these, simple pictures of a cat and dog will do. Prepare a name badge for each animal – *Mog* for the dog and *Pat* for the cat. Begin by introducing the two toys to the group. Hold up each of the name labels in turn. Encourage the children to try to blend the phonemes together to read each name.

2. Ask the children to guess which toy is called Mog and which is called Pat. Hopefully someone will notice the rhyme and deduce that it is Pat the Cat and Mog the Dog. Allow that child to come out and stick each badge on the correct toy.

3. Hold Mog in front of you. Choose a child to stand opposite you holding Pat. Instruct the children to listen really carefully. Say a word which ends in the *at* or *og* rhyme. Ask the children to decide whether the word rhymes with Mog or Pat and then stand beside the correct animal. Repeat with different *at* and *og* words. Make sure everyone has a turn holding Pat or Mog.

4. Once the group has got the hang of this activity, target individual children. This will challenge all the children to think for themselves and not just follow the crowd!

Independent work

● Organise the group so that they are sitting in pairs. Each pair will need a copy of the gameboard on the photocopiable sheet opposite, Mog the Dog and Pat the Cat counters, dice, two whiteboards or paper and pens. Ask the children to decide whether they are going to be Pat or Mog. Tell them to write the name of the animal they are going to be at the top of their whiteboard. Instruct the children to pick up their counters and put them on the space labelled *Start*. Outline how to play the game. (Before you explain the rules you may wish to read and discuss the words on the board with the group.) Direct the children to take it in turns to shake the dice and move that number of spaces around the board in the direction shown by the arrows. If someone lands on a word that rhymes with their chosen name, they can write the word on their whiteboard. The first player to collect a rhyming string of five different words is the winner – providing they can blend the phonemes to read the CVC words!

Further support

● Adapt the game to practise other rhyming strings, for example: *Len the Hen* and *Mig the Pig*.
● Play *og* and *at* 'Pairs' or 'Snap' with simple picture or CVC word cards.
● Play a rhyming strings game based on the card game 'Rummy'.

Plenary

● Pass the toys around the circle. Ask each child to say a rhyming word to generate a rhyming string.

Mog the Dog and Pat the Cat

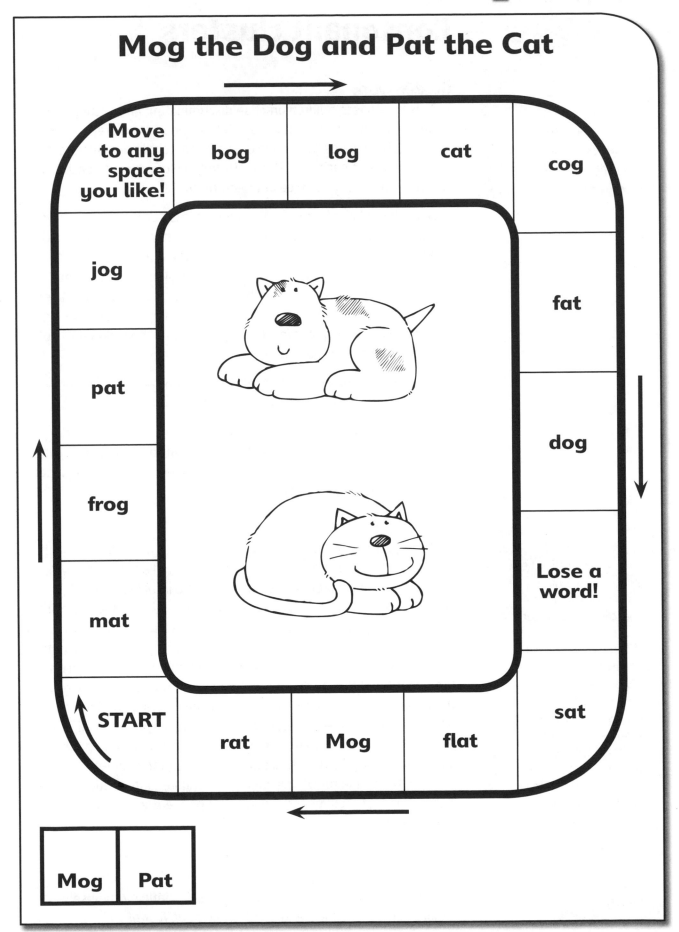

Move to any space you like!	bog	log	cat	cog
jog				fat
pat				dog
frog				Lose a word!
mat				sat
START	rat	Mog	flat	

Mog	Pat

50 LITERACY HOURS FOR LESS ABLE
LEARNERS: Ages 5-7

Consonant clusters

Objective
Y1. T2. W3.
To discriminate, read and spell words with initial consonant clusters.

Guided work

1. This lesson lets children practise discriminating and writing the initial consonant clusters in words. Before the session prepare a set of six large sound cards. Write one of the initial consonant clusters *bl, pl, gl, fl, sl* and *cl* on each card. Use a different colour to write each sound to emphasise the difference between them.

2. Begin by holding up one of the sound cards, for example, *bl*. Ask the children to blend the phonemes together to read the consonant cluster. Then challenge the group to think of as many words as they can that begin with that sound, for example: blue, black, blossom. Repeat this process for each of the cluster cards in turn. Try to keep this introductory activity pacy and fun. Whenever a suitable verb is suggested (for example, <u>*sl*</u>ide, <u>*bl*</u>ow, <u>*gl*</u>ide), allow the children to get up and demonstrate the action.

3. Display the sound cards, so that the children can refer to them throughout the rest of the lesson.

4. Play a 'Show me' game. Hold up one of the picture cards on the photocopiable sheet opposite. Ask the children to identify the cluster at the beginning of the word and write it on their whiteboard. Repeat this activity for the remaining pictures.

Independent work

● Play a game with the whole group working either individually or in pairs. Shuffle the picture cards and place them in a pile face down. Ask each of the children to choose one of the initial consonant clusters and write it on their board. Take the card from the top of the pile and slowly turn it over to reveal the picture to the group. Award a point to any children who have written and can correctly identify the cluster that represents the sound at the beginning of the word on their board. Tell the children to write a different consonant cluster on their board. Reveal the next picture and again award points to anyone who has guessed the correct sound. Continue playing until all the pictures have been turned over. Ask the children to count up how many points they have to find out who has won the game.
● If you have time remaining, divide the children into groups of two or three and let them play the game independently. Each group will need their own set of picture cards.

Further support
● Ask the children to help a puppet who is having difficulty pronouncing initial consonant clusters correctly.
● Let the children use the picture cards to play 'Pairs' or 'Snap', calling, 'Pair!' or, 'Snap!' whenever two pictures which begin with the same consonant cluster are put down together.
● Make a word card to go with each of the pictures. Ask the children to match the words to the pictures.
● Adapt the activities to teach or reinforce other initial or final consonant clusters.

Plenary

● Ask the children to choose a book and sit quietly by themselves looking for words which begin with *bl, cl, sl, gl, fl* or *pl*.

Consonant clusters

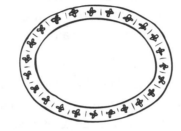

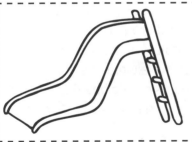

50 LITERACY HOURS FOR LESS ABLE LEARNERS: Ages 5-7

Long vowel phonemes

Objectives

Y1. T3. W1.
To learn the common spelling patterns for each of the long vowel phonemes.

Y2. T2. W1.
To secure the reading and spelling of words containing different spellings of the long vowel phonemes from Y1.

Guided work

1. Tell the group to listen carefully as you say some different words: *mole, blow, coat, hole, flow*. Ask who can hear the sound which is in every word. Repeat the words if necessary, emphasising the *oa* sound.

2. Ask the children to say the *oa* sound in different ways: quietly, surprised, loudly and so on. Play a quick game of 'Thumbs up' to check that the group can identify the phoneme *oa* in speech. Say a word, for example, *slope* or *feet*. Ask the children to decide if they can hear the *oa* phoneme and show a thumbs up or thumbs down accordingly.

3. Remind the children of the four ways of writing the *oa* sound: *o-e, oa, ow, oe*. Explain that, because it can be difficult to know which *oa* to use when spelling a word, you are going to teach them a trick to help them know when to use *oa* and *ow*.

4. Write two word lists on the board: *boat, coal, foal, goat* and *snow, bow, flow, glow*. Choose children to come out, read a word and underline the *oa* or *ow* phoneme. Ask the children to look closely at the position of the phonemes *oa* and *ow*. Hopefully someone will notice that *oa* occurs in the middle of words and *ow* at the end. (Make sure the children are aware that this is a general rule and there will be exceptions.)

5. Play the 'Boat or snow' game. Draw and label a boat and some snow on the board. Say a word that contains either *oa* or *ow*. If the children think they hear the *oa* sound in the middle, tell them to pretend to row a boat. If the *oa* sound occurs at the end of a word, the children make snow fall with their fingers. List the words on the board under the relevant picture so that the children can see if they were correct.

Independent work

● Give each child a laminated copy of the bingo board and six counters. Ask the children to choose six of the pictures and then write the words in the six spaces in the centre of their sheet. Remind the children that each of the words has *ow* at the end or *oa* in the middle. Allow the children time to write the words and check spellings as they go. Make a set of word cards for each of the pictures on the photocopiable sheet. Choose a caller to draw the words out of a bag. Play the game. The winner is the first player to cover all of their words and shout, 'Bingo!' If you think this is too challenging for your group, you could write the words on the boards before the lesson. Ask the children to read the words and join them to the correct picture.

Plenary

● Repeat the 'Boat or snow' game.

Further support

● Make the children aware of exceptions to the rule, for example: *toe* and *bowl*.
● Prepare *ow* and *oa* letter fans for everyone in the group. Say a word, for example, *boat*. Ask the children to hold up the correct vowel digraph.

Word bingo

◼ Choose words to fill in this board. Then play 'Bingo'.

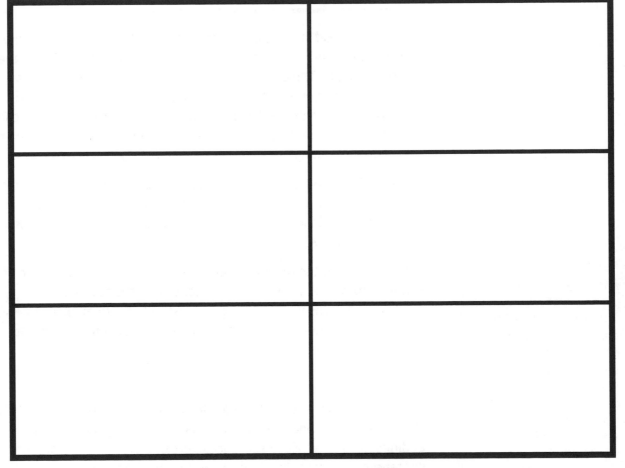

50 LITERACY HOURS FOR LESS ABLE
LEARNERS: Ages 5-7

Sentences

Objectives

Y1. T2. S6.
To use the term *sentence* appropriately to identify sentences in text.

Y2. T2. S9.
To secure the use of simple sentences in own writing.

Guided work

1. Write a sentence on the board, for example: *The girl is riding her bike.* Read the words together. Ask the children to tell you if the words on the board are a sentence. How do they know? If necessary, remind the children of the key features of a sentence.

- A sentence begins with a capital letter.
- A sentence ends with a full stop, question mark or exclamation mark.
- A sentence tells or asks you something and MAKES SENSE!

2. Give each child in the group a small card marked with a cross (x) on one side and a full stop on the other. Play 'Show me'. The rules of the game are simple. The children must listen carefully to what you say and decide whether or not they think it is a sentence. If they think you have said a sentence, the children must show the side of the card with the full stop marked on it. However, if they think the words you said were not a complete sentence, they must show the cross.

3. Have a practice together. Try to keep the game moving at a fast pace. At different points during the activity, stop and ask specific children to explain why they are showing you the full stop or cross. How do they know you did or did not say a sentence?

4. Depending on the reading ability of the group, you may wish to add variation to the game by writing sentences on the board for the children to read, as well as giving oral instructions. Remember to throw in some 'non-sentences' to challenge the children's ability to identify sentences correctly.

Independent work

- Give each child a copy of the photocopiable sheet opposite. Tell the children that you would like them to pair up the beginnings and endings to make sensible sentences. Ask the children to record the sentences. This could be either by writing the sentences down or by sticking the sentence beginnings and endings together. Encourage the children to read each sentence aloud to check that it makes sense.

Plenary

- Ask individuals to think of alternative sentence endings to those on the photocopiable sheet. The rest of the group could use their full stop cards to indicate whether they think the child has made a sentence or not.

Further support

- Highlight sentences during shared reading.
- During shared reading, challenge the children to predict a concealed sentence ending.
- Ask the children to compose simple sentences around a circle. The child who starts the sentence should stand up to signify a capital letter. Then, continue round the circle with each child adding one word to the sentence. Once the sentence is complete, the children should clap their hands or stamp their feet to indicate a full stop.

Sentences

The boy	is playing with her friend.
The cat	is riding his bike.
Mum and Dad	is running in the park.
The girl	is going to school with me.
My friend	are going to the shops.
A big dog	is in her bedroom.
The car	is climbing up a tree.
My sister	is red and very fast.

Capital letters and full stops

Objective
Y1. T2. S5.
To continue demarcating sentences in writing, ending a sentence with a full stop.

Y1. T2. S7.
To use capital letters for the personal pronoun 'I', for names and for the start of a sentence.

Guided work

1. Enlarge the picture on the photocopiable. Allow the children to look at the picture and encourage them to read the labels, using the picture cues and their phonic knowledge. Ask each child to say one sentence to describe the picture, for example: *The children are standing on the beach.* Write one of the sentences on the board, but miss out the capital letter and full stop. Ask the children whether you have written the sentence correctly. Hopefully someone will quickly spot your mistake. Allow that child to come out and correct the sentence.

2. Play 'Capital letters and full stops'. Explain that when you write a capital letter on the board everyone must stand up and when you write a full stop they must curl up tightly in a ball. Randomly write capital letters and full stops on the board. Instruct the children to watch carefully and make the appropriate body shapes.

3. Ask the children to think of other sentences for you to write about the picture. Tell them to perform the appropriate action at the beginning and end of each sentence to help you remember the capital letter and full stop.

4. Pick a child to say a sentence for you to write. Remind them to stand up to represent the capital letter at the beginning of their sentence and curl up and pretend to be a full stop when they have said the last word in the sentence. Write the sentence on the board. Repeat until you have written a sentence suggested by each member of the group. Then tell all the children to stand up. Read the text together, pointing to each individual word. Each time a full stop is reached, the children should curl up tightly and then quickly stand up straight and tall to represent the capital letter at the beginning of the following sentence.

Independent work

● Ask the children to work with a partner to write their own description of the picture on the photocopiable sheet opposite. Explain that you would like the children to take it in turns to say a sentence for their partner to write down. Remind them to do the actions to help their partner remember to use a capital letter and full stop.

Plenary

● Ask the children to sit in a circle. Choose a child to go first. Tell them to stand up, say a sentence about the picture and then curl up in a ball. The next person should then stand say a different sentence and curl up. Continue until everyone has had a turn.

Further support
● To help the children remember to use capital letters and full stops, let them write them in a different colour.
● Repeat the plenary activity whenever you have a spare five minutes. Ask the children to say sentences to describe an object, picture or themselves.

Capital letters and full stops

◼ Read the sentences below. Write some more sentences to describe the picture. Remember to begin each sentence with a capital letter and end it with a full stop.

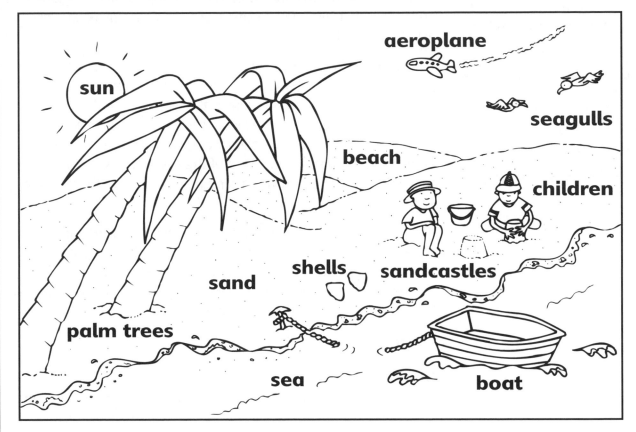

It is a hot day.

Two children are playing on the beach.

_____

_____

_____

_____

_____

Word order

Objectives
Y1. T3. S4.
To learn about word order, for example, by re-ordering sentences, predicting words from previous text, grouping a range of words that might 'fit', and discussing the reasons why.

Y1. T3. S6.
To reinforce knowledge of the term *sentence*.

Guided work

1. Prepare some A4-size word cards to make different sentences, for example: *We went to the park. The boy was going to school.*

2. Ask the children to define a sentence: it begins with a capital letter, ends with a full stop, question mark or exclamation mark and tells or asks you something.

3. Tell the children that you would like them to help you sort out a jumbled up sentence. Hand out the word cards for one of the sentences and a full stop to some of the group. Invite these children to stand in a line and hold their word cards up. At this stage it is important to make sure the children are not standing in the correct order. Read the words in the order of the children. Ask the children if they think what you read was a sentence. Did it make sense? Did it end with a full stop?

4. Tell the children that you would like them to order the words correctly to make a sentence. Ask them to consider who will be the first word in the sentence and who will show where the sentence finishes. Read the words together. Establish that what you have read has all of the characteristics of a sentence.

5. Repeat this activity to order the other jumbled sentences.

Independent work

● Ask each child to think of a sentence, write it down and then come and read it to you. Correct any spelling mistakes. Give everyone in the group a different coloured strip of thin card. Tell the children to copy their sentence neatly on to the strip of card and then cut it up into its component words and the full stop. Make a collection for the group. Ask the children to choose a set of coloured word cards, rearrange the words to make a sentence and then copy it down on to a piece of paper. Challenge the children to sort out and copy as many of the jumbled sentences as they can.

● In addition to the sentences the children devise, prepare before the lesson two or three extra jumbled sentences from the photocopiable sheet opposite. This will help avoid children having to wait around for the cards they need to be available.

Further support
● Write a sentence on the board with a word missing. Ask the children to say a word that they think would fit in the space.
● Write a selection of high frequency words on Post-it® Notes. Challenge the children to make as many sentences as they can, using only these words.

Plenary

● Allow the children to come out in turn and reveal the correct word order for their original sentence. Encourage the rest of the group to look on their sheet and see if they have unscrambled the sentences correctly. Remind the children to check their full stops and capital letters.

Word order

My friend plays with me .

I went to the shop with Dad .

Tom is a good boy .

I have two black cats .

The boy is playing in his garden .

Missing words

Objectives

Y1. T1–3. S2.
To use awareness of the grammar of a sentence to decipher new or unfamiliar words, for example, predict text from the grammar, read on, leave a gap and re-read.

Y1. T2. S3.
To predict words from preceding words in sentences and investigate the sorts of word that 'fit', suggesting appropriate alternatives.

Guided work

1. Organise the children in a circle. Begin by passing around the circle a large teddy bear wearing a scarf. Allow each child to spend a few moments looking closely at the bear. Next hide the bear under a piece of material. Ask each child to say one describing sentence about the bear, for example: *The bear is soft and fluffy*. Provide support for any child who has difficulty structuring their idea in a sentence.

2. Enlarge the sentences on the sheet opposite. Use Post-it® Notes to conceal the words written in bold. Put the first sentence on the board. Read the sentence with the children, pausing briefly at the concealed word. Re-read the sentence but this time stop at the missing word. Ask the children to predict what the missing word could be. Let them look at and touch the teddy to help generate ideas. Re-read the sentence filling the gap with some of the words suggested by the children. Consider which of the words are a suitable fit. Let one child come and reveal the covered word and read the complete sentence. Praise anyone who correctly guessed the word and anyone who suggested an appropriate alternative.

3. To keep the whole group actively involved during this activity, you might wish to let everyone write what they think the missing word is on an individual dry-wipe board.

4. Repeat this procedure for each of the sentences. When the missing word is not the last word in the sentence, explain to the children that it is important to read on to the end of a sentence before predicting the missing word.

Independent work

● Give everyone in the group a copy of the sheet opposite with the words in bold blanked out. Ask the children to complete each sentence by filling in the missing word. Encourage the children to use their knowledge of the correct grammatical order of words and their understanding of the context of the sentence. Ensure the children read each completed sentence to make sure the word they have added is a suitable fit. Reassure the children that sometimes there may be more than one word which is a suitable fit for the gap.

Plenary

● Play 'Guess the word'. Ask each child to write a sentence about the teddy on their whiteboard and then rub out a key word. Let one child read out their sentence, pausing at the missing word. Challenge the rest of the group to guess the missing word. Whoever guesses correctly first can be the next person to read their sentence out.

Further support

● Make a word bank of the missing words. Allow the children to select words from the word bank to complete the sentences.
● The whole activity could be done orally, if you feel it more appropriate for the group of children you are working with.
● During group and independent reading, encourage the children to read on, leaving a gap, and then re-read when trying to work out unfamiliar words.

Missing words

◧ Complete these sentences about Teddy.

The teddy bear is very **furry**.

He has a **black** nose.

The teddy has **two** ears.

The bear is wearing a **long** scarf.

If you stroke the bear, he feels very **soft.**

◧ Now write your own sentence.

Asking or telling

Objectives
Y1. T3. S7.
To add question marks to questions.

Y1. T3. T19.
To identify simple questions.

Guided work

1. Begin by asking the children some simple questions: *What is your favourite food? Who is your best friend? When is your birthday?* Encourage the children to answer each question in a full sentence: *My favourite food is...*

2. Discuss what you have been doing. Talk briefly about why people ask questions, for example, *to ask permission* or *to seek information.*

3. Ask the group to sit in a circle. Put a spinner labelled *ASK* and *TELL* in the centre of the circle. Tell the children that you are going to play a game called 'Ask or tell' which will help them find out information about each other. Explain that everyone will take turns to use the spinner. If the spinner lands on *TELL*, you must tell the rest of the group something about yourself, for example: *I am five.* If the spinner lands on *ASK*, you must ask someone else in the group a question to find out something about them, for example: *What is your favourite colour?* Allow all the children to have a few turns to spin and ask a question or tell the rest of the group a simple fact about themselves.

4. Gather the group around a whiteboard. Ask the children to suggest a *telling sentence* and an *asking sentence* (a question) for you to write on the board. Draw attention to the full stop demarcating the end of the telling sentence and the question mark at the end of the question. Read the sentences aloud with the group. Model how to change the tone of voice, depending upon whether you are making a statement or asking a question.

Independent work

● Give each child a large sheet of paper with the headings *Asking* and *Telling.* Ask the children to cut out the unpunctuated sentences on the photocopiable sheet opposite, read them aloud and then sort them under the appropriate heading. Instruct the children to add question marks to the questions and full stops to the statements.

Plenary

● Give each child a small piece of card and a felt-tipped pen. Demonstrate how to draw a full stop on one side of the card and a question mark on the other side. Let the children make their own card. Tell the children that you are going to spin the spinner where they cannot see it and ask or tell the group something, depending on what you spin. You would like the children to hold up their card each time, showing the question mark if they think you are asking a question and the full stop if they think you are telling them something.

Further support
● Play 'Show me' with the full stop/question mark cards (see 'Plenary'). Write a sentence on the board. Ask the children to decide whether it needs a full stop or a question mark.
● In pairs, children could pretend to be a reporter and interviewee. The reporter is only allowed to ask questions and must find out as much as they can about the other person.

Asking or telling

■ Sort out these sentences under the headings **Asking** and **Telling**. Remember to add question marks to the questions and full stops to the statements.

Can you skip

I love my mum and dad

Do you live in a house

On Sunday I went swimming

How old are you

Have you got a brother

I have a puppy called Charlie

What is your favourite colour

Sam likes to ride his bike

Are you a boy or a girl

My favourite sport is basketball

Asking questions

Objectives

Y1. T3. S7.
To add question marks to questions.

Y2. T3. S6.
To turn statements into questions, learning a range of 'wh' words typically used to open questions: what, where, when, who and to add question marks.

Guided work

1. Give each child a full stop/question mark card and play 'Show me' (see 'Asking or telling' on page 24).

2. Enlarge, copy and cut out the word cards on the sheet opposite. Read each of the words with the group. Stick them on the board so that the children can refer to them throughout the lesson.

3. Tell the children that you have invited a visitor into school to talk to them. Let them ask questions to try and find out who the person could be. Introduce Little Red Riding Hood into the hot seat. This could be you or another child wearing a cape and carrying a basket of groceries. Explain to the children that they can ask Little Red Riding Hood any questions they like to find out more about her, particularly her famous adventure with the wolf. Tell the children that, if they want to ask a question, they must hold up their question mark card. Encourage the children to start each question with one of the words on the board.

4. Encourage the whole group to listen carefully to the answers. After about five minutes of questioning, make an excuse why Little Red Riding Hood has to leave, for example: *Her Grandma is poorly again and she must hurry along to take her the groceries in her basket.*

Independent work

● Tell the children that you wanted to ask the wolf into school so that they could ask him some questions too, but the headteacher was frightened what the wolf might do! Allow the children to spend a few minutes discussing the terrible things the wolf might do. Explain that the wolf has said he will answer any questions over the telephone. Ask one of the children to think of a question they would like to ask the wolf. Write it on the board. Use a different colour to write the question mark. Reiterate that written questions always end with a question mark.

● Ask the children to write some questions for the wolf using the question words on the board. Instruct the children to use a coloured crayon to draw the question mark at the end of each question.

Further support

● Less able writers could record their questions on a tape recorder.
● Let the children write questions to ask each other or to ask you.

Plenary

● Sit on the floor and gather the group around you. Produce a telephone and choose a child to dial the wolf's number. Pretend to have a conversation where you are introducing yourself to the wolf. Let each child in the group have a turn to tell you one of the questions on their list. Ask the wolf the question and report his answer back to the group.

Asking questions

what

where

why

when

who

which

50 LITERACY HOURS FOR LESS ABLE
LEARNERS: Ages 5-7

Speech bubbles

Objectives

Y2. T2. S2.
To read aloud with intonation and expression appropriate to the grammar and punctuation.

Y2. T2. S7.
To investigate and recognise a range of other ways of presenting texts, eg speech bubbles, enlarged, bold or italicised print, captions, headings or sub-headings.

Guided work

1. Show the group an example of a speech bubble in a Big Book. Remind the children that, in picture books and comics, speech bubbles are often used as a way of showing that someone is speaking. The words inside a speech bubble tell you what a person is saying.

2. Tell the group that you are going to tell them a story they have heard before. Explain that, because you have not got a copy of the story book, you would like some of them to help you show what the characters are doing at different points in the story. Add that you will also be asking for volunteers to think about what different characters might be *saying* at different points in the story.

3. Retell a story the children are very familiar with, for example, 'Goldilocks and the Three Bears' (Traditional). At significant moments in the story, select children to stand up and make a freeze-frame of the action, for example: Goldilocks taking her first mouthful of porridge or Baby Bear looking shocked when he realises his chair is broken.

4. Ask whether anyone can think what the character(s) might be saying. Listen to different children's ideas and encourage them to speak with appropriate expression. Tell the whole story, pausing at suitable points to illustrate the scene and ask what the children think a character might be saying.

5. Prepare large laminated speech bubbles for each child. Show the children one of the pictures on the sheet opposite and choose someone to describe what is happening. What might the person in the picture be saying? Explain that you would like everyone to write down their idea in their speech bubble using a dry-wipe pen. Ask each child to stand up and read out the speech they have written, using the appropriate expression.

Independent work

● Give each child one of the pictures on the sheet opposite. Ask them to keep their picture hidden from the rest of the group. Explain that you would like everyone to look carefully at their picture and decide who they think might be speaking. Tell the children to write what they think that person could be saying in their speech bubble.

Plenary

● Collect the pictures and display them on the board. Ask each child in turn to come out to the front and read out the speech in their speech bubble. Challenge the rest of the group to look carefully at the pictures and decide which character they think is speaking.

Further support

● Working in pairs, one child could write a question in their speech bubble and their partner could give a response to the question.
● Provide pictures of people cut from newspapers and magazines to which the children can attach speech bubbles.

Speech bubbles

50 LITERACY HOURS FOR LESS ABLE
LEARNERS: Ages 5-7

Exclamation marks

Objectives

Y1. T1. S3.
To draw on grammatical awareness, to read with appropriate expression and intonation.

Y1. T3. S6
To reinforce, through reading and writing, knowledge of term 'sentence'.

Y2. T2. S2.
To read aloud with intonation and expression appropriate to the grammar and punctuation (sentences, speech marks, exclamation marks).

Y2. T2. S9.
To secure the use of simple sentences in own writing.

Further support
● Encourage the children to spot exclamation marks during shared, guided or independent reading. Model how to read aloud with expression appropriate to the grammar and punctuation.
● Play 'Show me'. The children must listen carefully to what you say and decide whether or not they think the sentence needs a full stop or an exclamation mark. Ask children to respond by tracing the appropriate shape in the air with their finger.

Guided work

1. Enlarge the speech bubbles on the sheet opposite. Read the text in each of the speech bubbles using a flat monotone voice. Hopefully the children will remark on the lack of expression. Focus on the text in one of the speech bubbles. Ask the children to suggest *who* might be speaking. Next discuss *how* the person might be speaking. Now read the text in each of the speech bubbles with the children, modelling the use of appropriate intonation and expression.

2. Look carefully at the speech bubble: *Come back here NOW!* Ask the children to justify how they knew to say the words in a bossy or loud tone. They will hopefully make reference to the use of capitals to suggest volume and the use of an exclamation mark to give emphasis.

3. Briefly discuss the children's knowledge of the use of exclamation marks. Can they explain why an exclamation mark has been used in the speech bubbles? Summarise that exclamation marks are used:

- to show that someone feels strongly about something
- to indicate surprise
- when someone is giving an order
- for emphasis, for example: BANG!

4. Now focus on the use of exclamation marks for emphasis when someone is giving an order. Ask the group to think of different orders grown-ups give to children. Encourage the children to contribute ideas from their own experience. Ask the rest of the group to draw an exclamation mark in the air at the end of each order suggested. Discuss the expression the children use when contributing their ideas.

Independent work
● Ask the children to write an order that a grown-up might give in each of the empty speech bubbles on the photocopiable sheet opposite. Tell them to make the orders sound as *bossy* as possible. Remind the children to put an exclamation mark at the end of each sentence to give emphasis to the order.
● To encourage the children to remember the exclamation mark, allow them to write it with a coloured crayon.
● Draw additional speech bubbles on the back of the sheet for children who finish quickly.

Plenary
● Ask different children to read out one or more of the orders in their list. Encourage the rest of the group to mark an exclamation mark in the air with their finger to demarcate the end of each sentence.

Exclamation marks

📕 Write an order in each of these speech bubbles, remembering to use exclamation marks.

50 LITERACY HOURS FOR LESS ABLE
LEARNERS: Ages 5–7

Connectives

Objectives

Y1. T2. S5.
To continue demarcating sentences in writing, ending a sentence with a full stop.

Y2. T1. S2.
To find examples, in fiction and non-fiction, of words and phrases that link sentences, for example, *after, meanwhile, during, before, then, next, after a while.*

Y2. T2. S9.
To secure the use of simple sentences in own writing.

Further support
● Say or write two simple sentences, for example: *James is excited. He is going to his friend's house for tea.* Ask the children to join the two sentences using the word *because*.
● Repeat the game using picture cards illustrating different locations, for example: the doctor's surgery, the school, the supermarket, the park and the zoo, to give the children further practice of joining sentences using *because*, for example: *I went to the ___ because ___.*

Guided work

1. Show the group each of the feelings cards on the sheet opposite. For each card, ask the children to describe the expression on the face and to identify the feeling it represents (1 happy, 2 sad, 3 excited, 4 angry, 5 scared, 6 upset). Encourage everyone to copy the facial expressions illustrated on the cards.

2. Shuffle the cards. Let one child choose a card and copy the facial expression. Ask the rest of the group if they can tell which card has been picked. Can they suggest reasons why a person might feel like this? For example, a person might feel *scared* if they were lost or *angry* if something had been stolen from them. Repeat this activity until all of the feelings cards have been selected and discussed.

3. Play a game using a 1-6 die and the picture cards. Ask a child to roll the die, take the appropriate card and show it to the group. Provide the opening of a sentence for the children to complete, eg: *Harry was feeling excited because…* Let everyone in the group have a turn and each time provide the sentence start, including the word *because*.

4. Write *because* on the board and explain that *because* is a special joining word which can be used to join two sentences together to make one longer sentence. The children may be able to suggest other joining words they know at this point (for example: *and, but* or *then*). Explain that *because* is used to join two sentences when the second sentence answers the question *why?* Illustrate with a couple of examples, for example: *Sam is feeling upset. He has lost his ball. Why was Sam upset? It was <u>because</u> he had lost his ball.* Show how these two sentences can be joined with the word *because* to make one longer sentence: *Sam is feeling upset because he has lost his ball.*

Independent work

● Ask the children to write simple sentences about different members of the group, including a feeling word from the picture cards and using the joining word *because* in each sentence. You may wish to prepare a simple writing frame to structure the children's writing:
    Mitchell is happy (because) ___. Angus is scared ___ ___.

Plenary

● Allow each child to read out one of the sentences they have written. To encourage the rest of the group to listen carefully, ask the speaker to omit the feeling word from their sentence. Ask the other children to guess which feeling is being described.
● Spend a few minutes teaching the children a simple strategy for spelling *because*.

Connectives

1.

2.

3.

4.

5.

6.

50 LITERACY HOURS FOR LESS ABLE
LEARNERS: Ages 5-7

Natalie Noun

Objectives

Y1. T3. W8.
To make collections of personal interest or significant words.

Y2. T1. W10.
To build individual collections of personal interest or significant words.

Guided work

1. Greet the group in role as Natalie (or Nigel) Noun, carrying a net bag containing a set of the noun cards from the sheet opposite. Describe yourself to the children. Your name is Natalie (or Nigel) Noun. You have a very important job - looking after words.

2. Explain that there are so many different words that you could not possibly look after them all by yourself, so your two good friends, Annie (or Alan) Adjective and Vernon (or Veronica) Verb, help you. Each of you is responsible for taking care of a different group of words. Tell the children that you are in charge of looking after a special group of words called *nouns* or *naming* words.

3. Show the children your bag and ask them to try and guess some of the words that might be inside it. Explain that a noun is a word which names something that you can see or touch. Inevitably some children will suggest words that are not nouns, for example, *purple* or *went*. Challenge these children to bring you *a purple* or *a went* to help them understand that these are not words which *name* objects.

4. Ask children to take a noun out of the net. Read the words together.

Independent work

● Tell the children that you would like them to help you do a very important job. Organise the children to work in twos or threes. Give each group a small net bag (empty orange or lemon nets are ideal for this) and some squares of card the same size as your noun cards. Each net should be labelled with one of the category cards on the sheet opposite: *food, animals, toys* or *clothes*. Instruct the children to make a set of noun cards to go in their net. Ask them to draw a picture and then have a go at spelling the word underneath. Emphasise that all of the cards should show both a picture and a label and that each child should try to produce a different noun card.

Plenary

● Collect up the nets and then redistribute them so that each group has a different net. Spread all the cards the children have made in the centre of the table. Challenge the children to find all the nouns which belong in their bag as quickly as they can. Alternatively, read out the words on the cards and ask the children to put up their hands if they think a word belongs in their net.

● Thank everyone for their help and say that you will visit again soon. Tell the children that you will let your friends, Annie Adjective and Vernon Verb, know how helpful the children have been. Hopefully, Annie Adjective and Vernon Verb will come and visit too!

Further support
● Play 'Spot the odd one out'. Display a selection of nouns and one word that is not a noun. Can the children identify the odd one out?
● Identify and highlight nouns during shared reading.

Nets of nouns

cake

house

tree

car

dog

cup

sun

boy

umbrella

● **FOOD**

● **ANIMALS**

● **CLOTHES**

● **TOYS**

50 LITERACY HOURS FOR LESS ABLE
LEARNERS: Ages 5-7

Annie Adjective

Objectives

Y1. T2. S5.
To continue demarcating sentences in writing, ending a sentence with a full stop.

Y1. T2. S7.
To use capital letters for the personal pronoun 'I', for names and for the start of a sentence.

Y2. T1. W5.
To read on sight and spell approximately 30 more words from Appendix List 1.

Guided work

1. Come into the session in role as Annie (or Alan) Adjective wearing an apron and carrying a bag containing each of the different fruits illustrated on the sheet opposite. Stick word cards displaying the adjectives *orange*, *yellow*, *green* and *red* on the front of the apron.

2. Remind the children, if necessary, that like your two friends, Natalie (or Nigel) Noun and Vernon (or Veronica) Verb, you are responsible for looking after an important group of words. You are the person in charge of the special group of words called *adjectives*. Describe in simple terms what adjectives are: a group of words that describe things and help to make writing more interesting.

3. Tell the children that you are a bit upset, because on your way to school this morning you were caught in a storm. Most of the adjectives on your apron were blown away in the wind! Prompt the group to read out the words left on your apron. Ask the children to think of things these colour words could be used to describe.

4. Request that the children help you to make some new adjective cards to stick on your apron. Take a piece of fruit out of your bag. Choose someone to hold the fruit. Ask them to look at it closely and think of a word to describe it. Write the adjective on a sticky label and let the child who thought of it come and stick it on your apron. Let the children take turns to think of an adjective until everyone has had a go. Encourage them to consider what the fruit looks like, how it feels, even how it tastes. Read all of the adjectives together. Thank the children for their help and praise their efforts.

Independent work

● Put the pieces of fruit on the table. Give each child a copy of the sheet opposite. Ask them to look carefully at the different fruits and then to use the words at the top of the sheet and the adjectives on your apron and in the box to write at least one sentence describing each fruit. Model a sentence on the board, for example: *The apple is hard*. Remind the children to begin each sentence with a capital letter and end it with a full stop.

Further support

● Limit the adjectives used in the written activity to colour words.
● Highlight examples of interesting adjectives in shared and guided reading.

Plenary

● Let the children taste one or more of the fruits and suggest adjectives that describe what they taste like. Remember to check for any allergies first.
● Ask the children to use adjectives to make a sentence more interesting, for example: *He ate a banana* could become *He ate a delicious banana*.

Annie's adjectives

◣ Try to use some of Annie's adjectives in your writing about these fruits.

apple   **banana**   **orange**   **strawberry**   **lemon**

The apple is _____

_____

_____

_____

_____

_____

_____

yellow	red	green
orange	hard	shiny
smooth	soft	curved
crisp	round	

50 LITERACY HOURS FOR LESS ABLE
LEARNERS: Ages 5–7

Synonyms

Objectives

Y1. T3. W8.
To make collections of personal interest or significant words and words linked to particular topics.

Y2. T3. W10.
To use synonyms and other alternative words/phrases that express same or similar meanings; to collect, discuss similarities and shades of meaning and use to extend and enhance writing.

Further support

● Play a game where the children split into two teams. Label each team with an adjective, for example, *big* and *small*. Pull synonyms for these two words out of a bag. The children should put their hands up if they think the word belongs to their team. The team that collects five words first wins.
● During shared reading, challenge the children to think of alternative adjectives.
● Choose a noun to describe, for example, giant (*big*, *huge*, *enormous* and so on).

Guided work

1. At the beginning of the session, greet the class in role as a very subdued Annie (or Alan) Adjective. You need to be wearing an 'adjective apron' (any plain apron) with the word *big*, or any other word overused by the group, attached in the middle.

2. Tell the children that you are very upset. You have received a lot of letters from teachers all over the country complaining that, when the children in their class write stories or poems, they often sound really boring. The teachers think it is your fault for not providing enough interesting adjectives for the children to use when they are writing.

3. Pretend to read out a passage of writing from one of the letters you have received, for example: *The big giant lived in a big castle in a big wood. He had a big wife and a really big dog.* Ask the children if they can explain to you what is wrong with this piece of writing. Hopefully, they will spot the problem straight away and tell you that the repetition of the word *big* throughout the passage makes the writing sound boring. The children may start to suggest alternative words and phrases without any prompting. If not, make an appeal to the group to help you think of other adjectives which mean *big*. Write each appropriate suggestion on a sticky label and ask the child who thought of it to come out and stick the label on your apron.

4. Now read the passage again, substituting the word *big* with the alternatives the children have come up with. Discuss with the children how the text sounds much more interesting now. Notice that the meaning of the text has not changed.

Independent work

● Tell the group that you would like them to help you make some word banks that you can send into schools to help other children make their writing more interesting. Write on the board some of the other words teachers have complained about children overusing, for example: *nice*, *pretty* and *small*. Demonstrate the task to the group. Write the word *big* on an enlarged copy of the photocopiable sheet. Write some of the synonyms thought of by the group on the lines around the edge. Now give each child their own word bank to fill in. Let them choose a starting adjective from the list on the board.

Plenary

● Collect up the word bank sheets. Choose one of the word banks and read the synonyms out. Ask the children to decide which of the words on the board they think these words are synonyms for.

Synonyms

■ Choose a word and make your own synonym word bank.

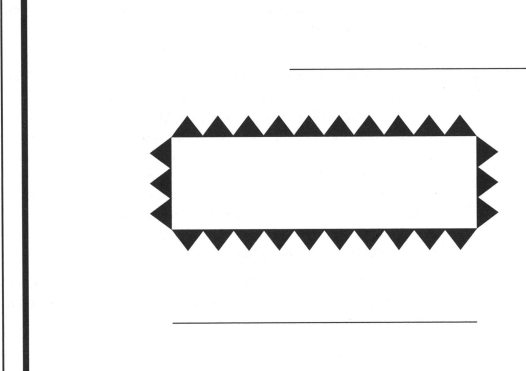

WORD BANK

small

tiny

little

short

Proper nouns

Objectives

Y1. T3. S5.

To learn other common uses of capitalisation, for example, for personal titles (*Mr, Miss*), headings, book titles, emphasis.

Y1. T2. W6.

To read on sight about 30 more words from Appendix List 1.

Y2. T1. W5.

To read on sight and spell approximately 30 more words from Appendix List 1.

Guided activity

1. Greet the group in role as Natalie (or Nigel) Noun. Make sure you are carrying your net of nouns! (See 'Natalie Noun' on page 34). You will also need to put a small net bag inside the large net. The smaller net needs to be a different colour or have some ribbon attached to it to make it look a bit special. The net should contain seven word cards with the days of the week written on them.

2. Ask if the children can remember who you are. Can anyone recall what is special about the words you carry in your net? If necessary, remind the children that it is a group of words called *nouns* or *naming* words. Tell the group they were so good last time you visited that you have bought your special net to show them. Ask for a volunteer to come and take the special net from the larger net.

3. Explain to the children that this bag is where you keep very important nouns called *proper nouns*. Ask the children in turn to carefully take one of the special nouns out of the bag, read it and then peg it on the washing line. Once all the words are displayed on the line, encourage the children to say what all of the words have in common (they all begin with a capital letter). Order the days of the week correctly. Explain that the days of the week belong to a special group of nouns which you must always write with a capital letter, even if they occur in the middle of a sentence. Other examples include people's names and place names.

4. Tell the children that their names belong to this group of words. Invite all the children to write their names on a card and come and put it in your special net.

Independent work

● Give each child a copy of the sheet opposite. Tell the children that the child who wrote it is very forgetful and hardly ever remembers to use capital letters in his writing. Explain that today you would like the children to pretend they are teachers. Instruct them to read the text and then use a coloured pencil to put in all the missing capital letters. At this point, give a clear reminder that people's names and the days of the week always start with a capital letter, even if they occur in the middle of a sentence.

Plenary

● Write a list of four words on the board, for example: *apple, wednesday, car, emily*. Challenge the children to identify which of the four words should begin with a capital letter. Repeat for different word lists.

Further support

● Read the text with the children, before asking them to work independently to identify which of the words should start with a capital letter.

● Enlarge the text and complete the activity as a group.

Proper nouns

◼ Correct these sentences by adding capital letters.

sam's busy week

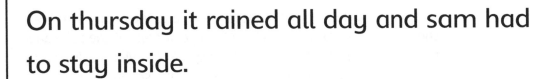

On monday sam went to school.

On tuesday it was sam's birthday.

sam went swimming on wednesday.

On thursday it rained all day and sam had
to stay inside.

friday was a hot day, so sam played on his bike.

sam went to his friend's house for tea on saturday.

All of sam's friends came to his party on sunday.

50 LITERACY HOURS FOR LESS ABLE
LEARNERS: Ages 5-7

Vernon Verb

Objectives
Y1. T2. S5.
To continue demarcating sentences in writing, ending a sentence with a full stop.

Y2. T2. S5.
To use verb tenses with increasing accuracy in speaking and writing, for example, *catch/caught, see/saw, go/went.*

Guided work

1. Make a set of word cards using the following words: *bounce, roll, throw, catch, kick* and *spin.* Put the cards and a small ball in a cloth bag marked with a large *V*.

2. Get into the character of Vernon (or Veronica) Verb wearing something distinctive so that the children will instantly recognise who you are, should you decide to play this character again at a later date. Introduce yourself to the children and tell them that you work with Natalie (or Nigel) Noun and Annie (or Alan) Adjective. Explain that you are responsible for looking after a special group of words called *verbs*. Describe in simple terms what a verb is: a word that tells you what something or someone does.

3. Show the children your verb bag. Explain that you have filled your verb bag with words that can be used to describe things that you can *do* with a ball. Tell the children that you would like them to guess the words that are in your bag. Take the ball from the bag and let everyone in the group demonstrate something they can do with it (for example, *roll* or *kick* it). Write the verb to describe the action each child does on the board. Then choose different children to take a word out of the verb bag, read it out and stick it on the board. Count up how many of the words in the bag the group guessed correctly.

4. Next, put out six objects that correspond to the pictures on the sheet opposite. Use a doll and a soft toy to represent the baby and the dog. Ask the children in pairs to spend a few minutes discussing what each of the things can do, for example: *a spoon can <u>stir</u>* and *a dog can <u>bark</u>.*

Independent work

● Ask the children to complete the sentences below each of the pictures on the sheet opposite by adding a verb which describes something that the animal or object can do. For example: *A pencil can draw.* Children who finish quickly could be challenged to underline the verb in each sentence with a coloured crayon.

Plenary

● Gather the group together. Write a sentence on the board about one of the objects you introduced in the lesson, for example: *A dog can bark.* Ask the children to identify the verb in the sentence. Choose someone to copy the verb on to a special card and put it into your verb bag. Repeat the activity until each child has put a verb in the bag. Thank the children for their help and disappear to mysteriously return as yourself!

Further support
● Provide a word bank of verbs that the children can copy under the correct picture.
● Ask the children to work in pairs. Give them just one object to focus on. Ask them to write as many verbs as they can think of which describe what that object can do.

Verbs

◼ What can these do?

spoon 	**pencil** 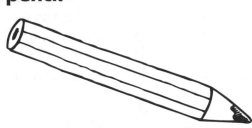
A spoon can _____	A pencil can _____
dog 	**hand** 
A dog can _____	A hand can _____
frog 	**baby** 
A frog can _____	A baby can _____

50 LITERACY HOURS FOR LESS ABLE
LEARNERS: Ages 5-7

Adding -ing

Objectives

Y1. T3. W6.

To investigate and learn spellings of verbs with '*ed* (past tense), '*ing*' (present tense) endings.

Y2. T2. S4.

To be aware of the need for grammatical agreement in speech and writing, matching verbs to nouns/pronouns correctly.

Guided work

1. Play a simple game of 'Charades'. Invite each child in turn to come out to the front, take a picture card (made from the sheet opposite) and mime the action illustrated. Ask the rest of the group to guess what action the child is miming. List the correct answers on the board: *singing, eating, brushing, sleeping, jumping, throwing, crying* and *pointing*. Read the words with the group. Encourage the children to remember who did each of the actions.

2. Ask the children to look at the words on the board. Can they spot what all the words have in common (they all end *i-n-g*). Remind the children of the sound these letters make when read together.

3. Allow each child to come out to the board and rub out the *-ing* at the end of one of the words. Then ask them to try to read the root verb which remains. Let the group perform the appropriate actions.

4. Next give each child an individual dry-wipe board and pen. Tell them that you are going to perform one of the actions on the cards and you would like them to write down a word to describe what you are doing. Ask: *What am I doing?* Allow everyone to read out their answer. It is likely that many of the children will simply have copied the appropriate verb from the board without adding *-ing*. Encourage the children to consider whether, for example, *sing* or *singing* sounds better. Repeat this activity for each of the action cards.

Independent work

● Give each pair of children their own set of action cards. Explain to the children that you would like one child to take a card and do the appropriate action. The other child should then write what they think the action is, by first copying the correct verb from the board and then adding *-ing*. Once they have done this, their partner can reveal the picture to indicate whether or not they have answered correctly. Work alongside individual children, correcting spellings as necessary. To make this activity more challenging, children could be asked to write their answer in a sentence, for example: *Joanne is eating. Roger is jumping.* Help the children to notice the construction of <u>*is* eating</u> and <u>*is* jumping</u>.

Plenary

● Allow each child to perform an action of their choice. Ask the rest of the group to guess what they are doing. Write the answers on the board. Choose a different child to add *-ing* to the verb root each time. Depending on the actions the children mime, you may have to explain that sometimes the spelling of a verb is modified when *-ing* is added.

Further support

● Write a shared alliterative poem about the children in the group, for example: *Sarah is shouting, Joe is jumping.*
● Write a simple timetable on the board to show what the children will be doing at different times of the day, for example: *writing, reading, playing, listening to a story.*

Adding -*ing*

50 LITERACY HOURS FOR LESS ABLE
LEARNERS: Ages 5-7

Adding -ed

Objectives
Y1. T3. W6.
To investigate and learn spellings of verbs with 'ed (past tense), 'ing' (present tense) endings.

Y2. T1. W7.
To use word endings, for example, 's' (plural), 'ed (past tense), 'ing' (present tense) to support their reading and spelling.

Y2. T2. S5.
To use verb tenses with increasing accuracy in speaking and writing, for example, *catch/caught, see/saw, go/went* and to use past tense consistently for narration.

Guided work

1. Read the text on photocopiable page 108 with the children. If you have already taught the lesson 'Character profile' on page 70, then the group will be familiar with Horrid Henry. If not, spend a few moments discussing with the children who Henry is. Talk about some of the naughty things he has been in trouble for at school today.

2. Ask the children to locate in the text the verbs that tell you what Henry did to William, Linda, Dave and Andrew. Write the words in a list on the board as they are identified by the children.

3. Ask the children to look carefully at the list of words. Can they spot what all the words have in common (they all end -*ed*). Remind the children of the sound these letters make when they are read together. Explain that -*ed* is added to the end of many verbs to show that something has happened before (that is, in the past). Choose different children to underline the -*ed* at the end of each of the words.

4. Challenge the children to find the other verbs ending -*ed* in the text as quickly as they can. Read the words and add them to the list.

5. Explain that you are going to mime an action and you would like them to try and guess what you are doing. Mime the action of kicking out at someone or something. Ask the children to say what you did (kicked someone). Write the word *kick* on the board. Choose a child to come and add -*ed* to the end of the word to show that it has already happened. Repeat this procedure for each of the actions listed on the sheet opposite.

Independent work

● Copy and cut out enough sets of the word cards on the sheet opposite for the children to share a set between two. Explain to the children that for this activity you would like them work with a partner. Ask them to look closely at the cards and match the past and present tense version of each verb. Once this task has been completed, they may use the cards to play a game of 'Pairs'. To make a pair, the past and present tense version of a verb must be turned over together.

Plenary

● Shuffle a set of word cards. Choose a child to take a card and say a sentence containing that word. A more challenging alternative would be for you to say some sentences using the verbs in the wrong tense, Ask the children to correct you by putting the verb in the correct tense.
● Ask the children to suggest some contrasting, less horrid -*ed* verbs, such as: *smiled, thanked, helped, laughed* and *shared*.

Further support
● Adapt the game by writing words which you know the children can read confidently on to the cards.
● Simplify the rules of the game by allowing children to make pairs by simply matching two past or two present tense verb cards.

Adding -ed

chew	tapped	burp	scream
trip	shove	screamed	pinched
tap	poked	tripped	burped
poke	shoved	chewed	pinch

50 LITERACY HOURS FOR LESS ABLE
LEARNERS: Ages 5-7

Plurals

Objective

Y1. T2. W8.
To investigate and learn spellings of words with 's' for plurals.

Guided work

1. Play a simple memory game with the group. Invite the children to sit in a circle and give one of them a small toy animal to hold. Ask the child to begin by saying: 'I went to the zoo and I saw one...' The child then adds the name of a zoo animal, for example, *elephant,* and passes the toy on to the next child in the circle. This child repeats the sentence and then builds on it by adding what they saw two of. Continue until everyone in the group has had a turn.

2. Tell the children that you would like them to help you write a list of all the animals they saw at the zoo. Begin by asking someone to tell you the first animal they saw (for example, *one elephant*). Say the word aloud as you write it on the board. Encourage different children to tell you the letters you need to write to represent particular sounds. Continue adding animal names to the list until all the children's suggestions have been recorded. Engage and maintain the children's attention during this shared writing activity by involving them in the writing process. Ask them to show you the letter or letters they think you need to write next on individual dry-wipe boards or by tracing letter shapes in the air with their fingers.

3. Read the list with the group. Tell the children to look carefully at the animal names to spot the odd one out. Can they say why the first animal is the odd one out? Explain that we can add the letter *s* to a noun to indicate that there is more than one of that particular thing. Model how *five bear, three girl* and *seven bird* do not sound correct. Say that we need to add an *s* to each of these nouns, because there is more than one of each thing.

4. Give each child a small piece of card. Tell them to write the letter *s* on one side of the card. Play a 'Show me' game using the picture cards on the photocopiable sheet opposite. Hold up one of the picture cards. Ask the children to say what it is a picture of. Tell them to hold up their *s* card if they can hear an *s* on the end of the word. Encourage the children to recognise that they will only hear an *s* if there is more than one of a particular object pictured.

Independent work

● Organise the children into small groups. Ask them to match the picture and word cards on the photocopiable sheet opposite and then use the cards to play 'Pairs'.

Plenary

● Repeat the 'Show me' game played in the lesson, asking the children to draw the letter *s* in the air with their finger.

Further support

● Ask the children to select the appropriate word card to complete a sentence, for example:
Sam has got three toy _____ (*cars*).

Plurals

star	stars	car	cars
flower	flowers	dog	dogs
tree	trees	apple	apples

50 LITERACY HOURS FOR LESS ABLE
LEARNERS: Ages 5–7

Syllables

Objective
Y2. T2. W5.
To discriminate, orally, syllables in multi-syllabic words using children's names and words from their reading, for example, *dinosaur, family, dinner, children.*

Guided work

1. Demonstrate to the children that, when you say a long word (for example, *dinosaur*) slowly like a robot, you can hear how it can be broken down into smaller parts. Say the word slowly emphasising each syllable: *di-no-saur.* Clap to mark each syllable. Tell the children that the smaller parts that you have broken the word down into are called syllables. Ask them to count the claps as you repeat the word to find out how many syllables it has. Challenge the children to count the syllables in a variety of different words. Encourage them to join in, saying the words and clapping the syllables with you.

2. Draw a chart with five columns on the board. Write the headings: *1 syllable, 2 syllables* and so on at the top of each column. Explain that you are going to work together to find out how many syllables each of the children's names can be broken down into. Ask the group to sit in a circle. Teach the children the words below.

> Clap your name.
> Clap your name.
> We'll count the syllables
> While you clap your name.

3. Sing the words together while passing a small object around the circle. The child holding the object at the end of the last line is 'it' and must say their name slowly like a robot clapping on each syllable. The rest of the group counts the claps to find the number of syllables. The child who is 'it' should write their name in the correct column on the board. Repeat the activity until all have had a turn. Encourage the children to look closely at the completed chart and answer questions, such as: *How many children have one syllable in their name?*

Independent work

● Organise the children to play in pairs the 'Syllables game' on the photocopiable sheet opposite. Each pair will need a racetrack, two different coloured counters and a set of the picture word cards.
● Instruct the children to shuffle the cards and place them in a pile face down. They must take it in turns to take a card from the pile. They must say the name of the fruit or vegetable slowly, count how many syllables it has and, if their opponent agrees, they move their counter that number of spaces around the track. The winner is the first player to move their counter around the track from start to finish.

Plenary

● Ask the children to quickly sort the cards into words with one, two or three syllables.

Further support
● Add variety to the guided activity by letting children tap out syllables on a range of simple percussion instruments.
● Make the 'Syllables game' easier by annotating the picture word cards. Use a different colour to represent each syllable, for example: *or-ange.*

Syllables game

apple

strawberry

banana

pineapple

pear

tomato

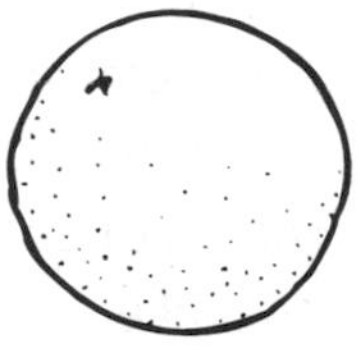

orange

carrot

grapes

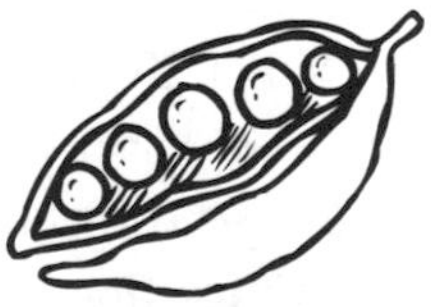

peas

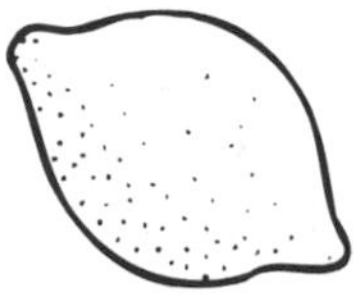

lemon

beans

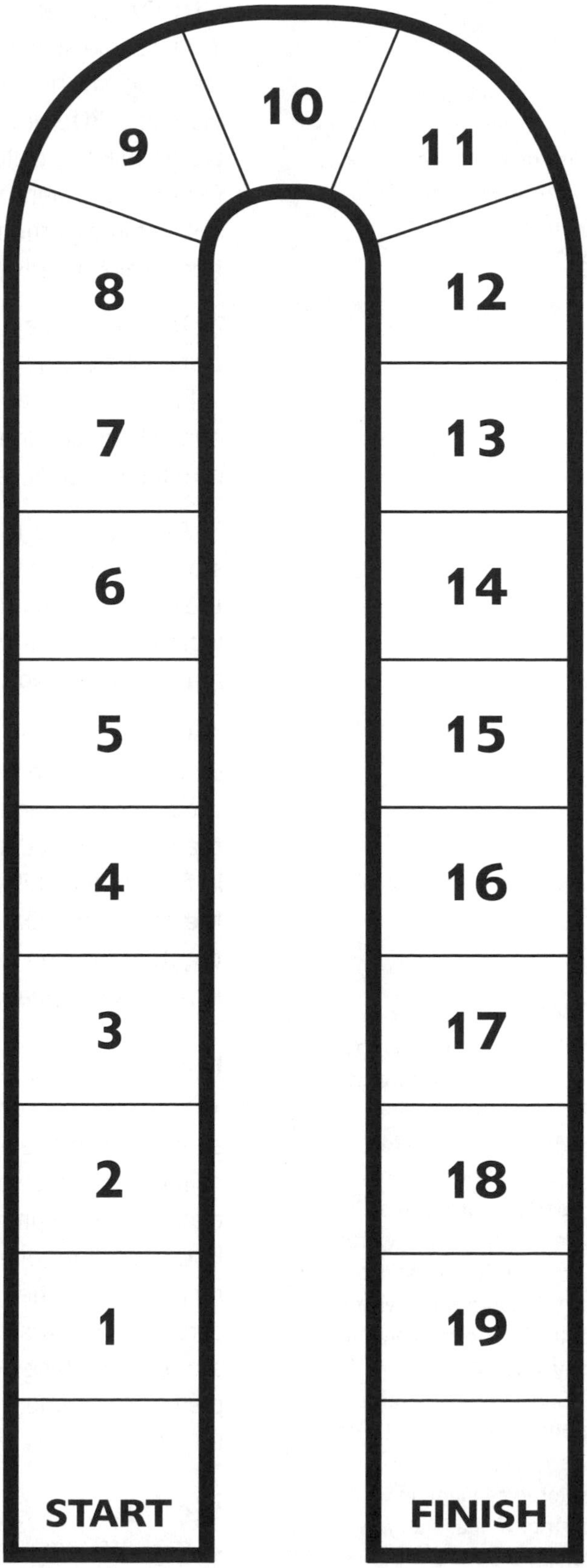

9

10

11

8

12

7

13

6

14

5

15

4

16

3

17

2

18

1

19

START

FINISH

50 LITERACY HOURS FOR LESS ABLE
LEARNERS: Ages 5-7

Compound words

Objective
Y2. T2. W4.
To split familiar oral and written compound words into their component parts, for example, *himself, handbag, milkman, pancake, teaspoon.*

Guided work

1. List some simple compound words on the board, for example: *handbag, sunflower* and *blackbird.* Write the component parts of each word in a different colour. Begin by asking the children to read the words. Ask the children if they notice anything unusual about them. Expect the children to focus on the different colours you have used, but encourage them to notice that each of the words is made up of two smaller words joined together.

2. Tell the children that these words belong to a special group called *compound words.* Explain that a compound word is one that can be split into two smaller words. Focus on each of the examples in turn and ask the children to say which two smaller words each of the compound words can be broken into.

3. Ask the group to try to think of other compound words. At this stage the children will probably find this difficult to do and are likely to suggest words that are not compound words. Write some of these words on the whiteboard and discuss with the children why they are not compound words.

4. Give each of the children in the group one of the picture word cards on the sheet opposite. Choose a child to come and stick their card on the board (this would work well on an interactive whiteboard) and read the word out loud. Repeat until all the picture word cards are displayed in front of the children. Say a compound word that can be made from the cards, for example: *lighthouse.* Select a child to come out and put together the two correct words which join together to make *lighthouse.* Repeat this activity until all of the cards are paired up.

Independent work

● Split the children into two small groups. Give each group a set of some or all of the picture word cards on the sheet opposite. Tell the children that they are going to use the cards to play 'Pairs'. Instruct each group to spread the cards face down in front of them and take it in turns to turn over two cards. If a child turns over two cards that can be joined together to make a compound word, they can keep the cards. If the cards cannot be joined to make a compound word, they are returned face down to the table and play passes to the next player. The game is over when all the cards have been correctly paired up. The winner is the player who has made the most words.

Plenary

● Say different compound words. How quickly can the children tell you into which two smaller words the compound words can be split?

Further support
● Encourage the children to spot compound words during shared reading. Highlight these words using a different colour to underline each of the smaller component words.
● Make different sets of picture word cards with the children. Use the cards to play 'Pairs' again.
● Give everyone in the group a picture word card. See how quickly the children can join up with a partner to make a compound word.

Compound word cards

 **house**

 **brush**

 bow

 **bird**

 light

 **hair**

 rain

 **lady**

 **flower**

 **fly**

 **bag**

 man

 **sun**

 **butter**

 **hand**

snow

Vowels and consonants

Objectives

Y1. T1. W4.
To discriminate and segment all three phonemes in CVC words.

Y1. T3. W9.
To learn the terms 'vowel' and 'consonant'.

Guided work

1. Prior to the session fill a bag with objects to use for the CVC sorting activity (point 4), for example: *a hat, pen, cup, pig* and so on.

2. Display the 26 letters of the alphabet in order. Mark the vowels in some way to make them stand out from the other letters.

3. Can the children tell you the sounds that the five letters you have highlighted make. Explain that the marked letters are called vowels and the rest of the letters are called consonants. Ask the children to count up how many of the letters are vowels and consonants. Starting with the letter *A*, point to each letter of the alphabet in turn for the children to say *vowel* or *consonant*.

4. Put five small hoops on the floor or table. Label each hoop with a different vowel. Show the children your bag and explain that each of the objects belongs in one of the hoops. Ask them to help you sort them correctly. Choose one of the children to come and take an object from the bag, for example, *a pen*. Instruct the children to listen very carefully as you say the word *pen*. Can they identify which of the five vowel sounds occurs in the middle of the word and put the pen into the appropriate hoop? Repeat this procedure until all the objects in the bag have been sorted correctly.

5. Encourage all the children to remain focused and involved, even when it is not their turn. You could ask them to write the medial vowel on a whiteboard or card or show you with a vowel letter fan.

Independent work

● Divide the children into groups of three - a caller and two players. Give each group two sets of different coloured counters, an enlarged copy of the gameboard on the sheet opposite and a bag containing the CVC picture word cards. Decide who is going to start. The caller takes a card from the bag and reads it to that child. The first player tries to identify the medial vowel sound and covers the letter representing that sound on the board with one of their counters. The next player has a turn. The caller continues to read a word to each of the players until someone has covered four vowels in a row. The winner swaps with the caller and play begins again. Depending on the reading ability of the children in the group, you may wish to prepare the word cards without the picture cues.

Plenary

● Show the children the letters of the alphabet in a random order and ask the children to say which are vowels and which are consonants.

Further support
● Simplify the sorting activity and game so that the children only have to distinguish between two vowel sounds, for example: *A* and *E*.
● Ensure the children see the vowels written in both upper and lower case.
● Play 'Vowel snap'.

Vowels and consonants game

a	i	e	i	u	o	a
o	a	o	i	e	a	o
u	o	i	a	o	u	e
e	i	e	a	a	i	e
u	a	u	i	u	e	o

hat	sun	bed	mug	six	nut	pot
pen	cup	pig	bin	cot	pan	rug
zip	ten	map	rat	peg	leg	cat
dog	bag	bud	hen	saw	pin	log

50 LITERACY HOURS FOR LESS ABLE
LEARNERS: Ages 5-7

Alphabetical order

Objective
Y1. T1. W2.
To practise and secure alphabetic letter knowledge and alphabetical order.

Guided work

1. Remind the children that in the alphabet the letters always occur in the same order. Chant or sing the alphabet together and point to each letter on an alphabet frieze as the children say its name.

2. Enlarge and cut out the 26 letter cards on the sheet opposite. Spread the letter cards out randomly in front of the children. Challenge the group to work together to arrange the letter cards in alphabetical order as quickly as they can. To avoid a mad scramble, ask the children to take it in turns to come and peg the next letter on a washing line. Once all the letters are pegged up, choose a child to say the letters in sequence to check for alphabetical order.

3. Tell the children to close their eyes. Remove one of the alphabet cards from the washing line. Ask the children to work out which letter you have hidden. The children could tell you the missing letter orally or show you by drawing it on a dry-wipe board.

4. To vary the activity, instead of taking a letter away, swap two letters over. Choose a child to come out and correct the letter order. Repeat until all children have had a turn.

Independent work

● Give each child an alphabet strip from the sheet opposite and a coloured counter. As you call out random letters, challenge the children to place their counter on that letter as quickly as they can. This will help to familiarise the children with the position of different letters in the alphabet.

● Ask the children to sit with a partner. Each pair of children will need one alphabet strip, sets of two different coloured counters and a set of letter cards placed upside down in the centre of the table. Explain the rules of the game. Each player takes a letter card from the central pile. Both letters are then located on the alphabet strip. The player whose letter comes first in the alphabet takes a counter and scores a point. Continue taking letters and locating them on the alphabet strip. The winner is the player who has collected the most counters when all the letter cards have been used.

● Once children have got the hang of the game, reorganise the group so that the children are playing the game in threes or fours and so have to compare the position of more letters. If some children find this too difficult let them plays in pairs.

Plenary

● Organise pairs of children to race to be the first to sort their letter cards into alphabetical order from A–Z.

Further support
● Instead of letter cards, put simple words into alphabetical order, for example: names, animals or topic words.
● Play alphabet games regularly to develop the children's understanding of alphabetical order. Use a timer to keep the games fast moving and the children motivated.

Alphabetical order

A	B	C	D	E	F	G	H	I	J	K	L	M	
a	b	c	d	e	f	g	h	i	j	k	l	m	

N	O	P	Q	R	S	T	U	V	W	X	Y	Z	
n	o	p	q	r	s	t	u	v	w	x	y	z	

A	B	C	D	E	F	G	H	I	J	K	L	M
N	O	P	Q	R	S	T	U	V	W	X	Y	Z

50 LITERACY HOURS FOR LESS ABLE
LEARNERS: Ages 5–7

Predictable and repeating patterns

Guided work

1. Enlarge a copy of photocopiable page 109. Share the story and invite the children to join in with the repeated line, *'But I don't want to go to bed!'* using appropriate expression. At the end, ask the children to recall the different activities that this character had to carry out. Discuss the children's own bedtime routines.

2. Read the text again with the group joining in. What do they notice about the way the story is written? Highlight the repeated phrases. Consider the tone used to give instructions and the use of capitalisation and bold text to give emphasis to the final line.

3. Tell the group that you would like them to work together to write a story called 'Teddy's Bedtime' based on the text you have just read. Introduce a teddy bear to the children. Explain that Teddy does not like going to bed, so his mum and dad have to get very bossy with him at bedtime. Have a little bag filled with props to represent all the things that teddy has to do to get ready for bed.

4. Encourage each child to come and take an object from the bag and say what activity they think it stands for. Next, ask the children to consider the order in which Teddy might carry out these activities. Stress that with any routine there is usually a logical order in which tasks are carried out, for example: *Teddy would have his milk before he cleaned his teeth.* Help the children organise themselves into a line in a suitable order according to their object or task.

5. Tell the story 'Teddy's Bedtime'. Ask the first child in the line to contribute the first two lines. For example: *Bedtime in five minutes! Tidy up your toys!* Let the rest of the group respond with: *But I don't want to go to bed!* Continue until you reach *Bedtime!* Depending on the number of children in the group, you may need to start from a different number of minutes.

Independent work

● Ask the children to keep hold of their props and remember the number of minutes they said. Give each child a copy of the sheet opposite. Explain that you would like everyone to write down their part of the story. Provide a word bank of number words.

Plenary

● Fasten the children's work together to make a book. Choose one child to act out the story with Teddy and the various props.

Bedtime

■ Write your line of the story. Draw a picture of what you have written.

'Bedtime in _____ minutes.'

_____

'But I don't want to go to bed!'

Traditional tale

Objectives

Y1. T1–3. T2.
To use phonological, contextual, grammatical and graphic knowledge to work out, predict and check the meanings of unfamiliar words and to make sense of what they read.

Y1. T3. T5.
To retell stories, to give the main points in sequence and to pick out significant incidents.

Guided work

1. Make an enlarged copy of photocopiable page 110. Conceal the title with a Post-it® Note. Read the text with the children. Encourage them to use their phonic knowledge to decipher any unfamiliar words. Model the use of appropriate intonation and expression. Ask the children if anyone thinks they know which story this dialogue is taken from. It is likely that most of the children will be familiar with the story of 'The Little Red Hen' (Traditional). Remove the Post-it® Note to reveal the title to the group.

2. Tell the children the full story of 'The Little Red Hen'. Ask the children to play the part of the animals and direct them to read out the shared text at the appropriate points in the story.

3. Explain that 'The Little Red Hen' is a traditional tale and many different versions of the story exist. Explain that, in each retelling, the main events and the order in which they occur remain the same, and it is only smaller details which vary. Briefly discuss any similarities and differences between this story and other versions the children may know. Ask the children to identify the different characters in the story and to comment on their behaviour and actions. Encourage the children to recall and describe the main incidents in the story in the correct order.

Independent work

● Organise the children to work in pairs. Give each pair a set of the picture cards on the photocopiable sheet opposite. Ask the children to discuss what is happening in each of the pictures. Instruct the children to arrange the picture cards in the order in which the events occur and then to retell the story using the picture cards as cues. Intervene where appropriate to help the children retell the story effectively, for example, by adding descriptive phrases and dialogue.

Plenary

● Say to the children that you are going to tell them a different version of the same story. Shuffle a set of the picture cards and ask a child to come out and choose one. Begin with *Once upon a time...* and then incorporate the incident illustrated on the card. Let a different child select a card to determine the next event in the story. Children will hopefully find the resulting story quite humorous and will also appreciate the importance of recalling incidents in the correct sequence. Discuss with the children why it is important to sequence the main incidents correctly, for example: the little Red Hen cannot cut the wheat if she has not planted the grain!

Further support

● If the children find it difficult to retell the entire story in sequence, simplify the activity. Give each child one of the picture cards. Ask them to stand in the order that the events occur in the story. Retell the story collectively with each child describing the incident represented on their card. Consider how this retelling differs from the version you told at the beginning of the lesson.

Traditional tale

Story box

Guided work

1. Prepare an exciting story box or bag. Place a selection of interesting objects into the box, for example: a feather, a toy animal, a shell or a key. Copy, colour and laminate the setting cards from the sheet opposite.

2. Begin by showing the group the box and each of the objects inside it. Tell the children that this is called a story box. Explain that anyone can use the story box to tell a story, but there is one special rule that the storyteller must always follow. They must incorporate three of the objects in the box into their story.

3. Demonstrate to the group how to use the box. Hold up each of the setting cards and ask a child to choose one of the cards to determine the setting for the story. Start telling a story. Set the scene and introduce the main characters. Name the main characters after children in the group to instantly grab their interest. Incorporate one of the objects into the story. For example, *One sunny morning two children, Harry and Abbie, were walking along the beach when they noticed a beautiful <u>shell</u> lying on the sand.* Ask someone to hold the shell as you continue the story. Encourage different children to help you shape the story by asking questions for example: *What do you think might happen next? What do you think Abbie said when she realised it was a magic shell? What do you think she might use the magic shell to wish for?* Incorporate some of the children's suggestions into the story.

4. At a significant point in the story, stop and discuss with the group what has happened so far. Encourage them to identify how the main events in the story link to the plot, setting and characters.

Independent work

● Working in pairs, ask the children to think of a suitable ending for the story. Allow each pair of children to choose an object from the story box to influence the ending they devise. Ask them to discuss their ideas together and then to tell their ending to another pair of children. Emphasise how the end of the story should be based on the plot so far, and the characters and setting should not change.

Plenary

● Choose a child to retell the whole story, adding on the ending they devised with their partner. Ask the rest of the group to suggest an appropriate title for the story. Write the best suggestion on a strip of card and put it in the story box. Allow the children to use the story box to retell the story at a later date.

Story box

Story opening

Objectives
Y1. T1. T5.
To describe story settings and incidents and relate them to own experience and that of others.

Y1. T2. T14.
To represent outlines of story plots using, for example, captions, pictures, arrows to record main incidents in order.

Guided work
1. Read the story opening on photocopiable page 111 with the children. Discuss the main points of the text. Who is the main character in the story? Why was Billy feeling fed up? Encourage the children to empathise with Billy's feelings of frustration that he is not allowed to do any of the things he wants to do. Ask the children to suggest some of the things they think Billy would like to do but is not allowed to. Re-read the final section of the text. Ask the children to suggest why 'NEVER NEVER' is written in upper-case letters. Establish that there might be something dangerous or frightening beyond the gate that Billy's mum is trying to protect him from.

2. Show the group the sheet opposite. Discuss the illustration in the first box, which shows Billy looking longingly towards the garden gate. Explain that you would like everyone to write a story about Billy and that this picture will represent the beginning of their story. Ask the children to imagine they are Billy. Encourage them to slouch down in their chair and look really fed up! Put a chair or box in front of them to represent the garden gate. Tell the children to pretend to creep out of the house, really quietly so that their mum will not notice. When they reach the 'garden gate', ask the children to stop and suggest what might lie beyond it (for example: monsters, dragons, a dark, gloomy forest, fairies and goblins).

3. Say to the children that you would like them to draw a picture of what they think Billy sees behind the gate in the second box. Allow the children a few moments to complete this task. Let all the children describe their picture to you or to a partner.

4. Tell the children that you would like them to think about what might happen to Billy next in their story. For example, if Billy met a monster behind the garden gate, it might eat him up. Allow them a few minutes to discuss their ideas before drawing pictures to represent them in the third box. Ask one of the children to tell their story by saying a sentence about each of the pictures they have drawn.

Independent work
● Ask the children to complete the page opposite by writing a simple sentence beside each of the pictures they have drawn.

Plenary
● Let the children read their completed storyboards to a partner or to the rest of the group.
● Read a little more of *The Minpins* by Roald Dahl (Puffin), if you have a copy, to see what Billy did.

Further support
● Create a group story. Compose and write sentences with the children as a shared writing activity.
● Prepare some pictures illustrating alternative middles and endings to the story. Ask the children to sequence the pictures and tell the stories orally.

Story opening

■ Write a story about Billy.

50 LITERACY HOURS FOR LESS ABLE
LEARNERS: Ages 5-7

Character and dialogue

Objectives

Y1. T2. T9.
To become aware of character and dialogue, for example, by role-playing parts when reading aloud stories or plays with others.

Y1. T3. S3.
To read familiar texts aloud with pace and expression appropriate to the grammar, for example, pausing at full stops, raising voice for questions.

Y1. T3. S5.
To learn other common uses of capitalisation, for example, for personal titles (*Mr, Miss*), headings, book titles, emphasis.

Guided work

1. Recall the story of 'Goldilocks and the Three Bears' (Traditional). Use three different sized bears, bowls, spoons and any other props you have available to help you as you read the text on photocopiable page 112 to the children. Model the use of appropriate expression and intonation for each of the characters' voices.

2. Explain that you used the clues given in the text to determine the voice you used for each of the bears: *a deep, gruff voice* for Daddy Bear, a *soft, low voice* for Mother Bear and a *shrill, high voice* for Baby Bear. Ask the children if they would have known what kind of voice to use if the author had not included this information in the text. Discuss how the use of capital letters gives emphasis to certain words in the dialogue. Consider how the author varies the size of the text to indicate how loudly the bears are speaking.

3. Re-read the passage to the group. Ask the children to join in with the speech. Encourage them to read with appropriate expression for each of the bears and to raise their voices a little at the end of each sentence because they are asking a question.

4. Copy and cut up the text on the sheet opposite. Organise the children into three small groups. Give each group one of the dialogue cards, ask them to decide which of the bears is speaking and practise reading the dialogue together with appropriate expression. Ask each group to perform to rest of the children.

Independent work

● Give each group one of the teddy bears. Ask them to decide what they think their bear would have said when it discovered that Goldilocks had been sleeping in its bed. Provide whiteboards or paper and pens so that one group member can write their idea down.
● Discuss the children's ideas as a group. Have they used capitalisation for emphasis and remembered a question mark at the end of the sentence?

Plenary

● Instruct the children to sit in a circle. Explain that you would like them to role-play the parts of the three bears as you retell the story. Choose three children to hold the teddies. Start retelling the whole story and pause each time you reach a point in the story where one of the bears speaks. Let the child holding the appropriate bear add the dialogue and then pass on the bear to someone else in the group to ensure everyone is involved in the activity.

Further support

● Encourage less confident children by organising the children to work with a partner during the plenary.

Character and dialogue

'WHO'S BEEN SITTING IN MY CHAIR?'

'WHO'S BEEN SITTING IN MY CHAIR?'

'WHO'S BEEN SITTING IN MY CHAIR AND BROKEN IT ALL TO BITS?'

Characters

Objectives

Y1. T2. T8.

To identify and discuss characters, for example, appearance, behaviour, qualities; to speculate about how they might behave; to discuss how they are described in the text; and to compare characters from different stories or plays.

Y1. T2. T15.

To build simple profiles of characters from stories read, describing characteristics, appearances, behaviour with pictures, single words, captions, words and sentences from text.

Further support

● Modify the above activities to suit different stories the group know well.

● Prepare a simple character profile to read to the children. Ask them to guess the character being described.

● Hot-seat different characters from stories the children know well.

Guided work

1. This lesson is based on 'Jack and the Beanstalk' (Traditional). The group needs to be very familiar with the characters and events in the story, so begin the lesson by asking the children to help you recall what happens, or by reading a version of the tale to the group.

2. Invite the children to help you compile a list of all the characters in 'Jack and the Beanstalk' – that is, *who* is in the story. Once the list is complete, ask the children to identify who they think are the main characters in the story.

3. Ask the children some questions to generate a simple discussion about the appearance, behaviour and qualities of the main characters. Possible questions could include: *What do you think Jack looked like? How do you think Jack felt when he saw the Giant? How do you know that Jack was brave?*

4. Tell the children that you have made a set of words to describe the main characters in the story. Unfortunately you dropped them on your way to school this morning and now the cards are all mixed up. Explain that you would like the children to help you sort the words into those which describe Jack and those which describe the Giant. Read out one of the words, for example, *brave*. Tell the children that, if they think the word describes the Giant, they must stand up tall like a Giant. However, if they think the word best describes Jack, they must pretend to climb a beanstalk.

5. Encourage individual children to justify their choices by referring to events in the story, for example: *I think Jack was brave because he kept climbing back up the beanstalk, even though he was frightened of the Giant.* Repeat until all the words have been sorted correctly.

Independent work

● Tell the children that you would like them to draw a picture of either Jack or the Giant and then write about the character using some of the describing words. Depending on the children's ability, you could ask them to either annotate their pictures with some of the adjectives or use the adjectives to write simple descriptive sentences about the character they have chosen.

Plenary

● Challenge the children to think of other adjectives to describe a character from a different story that they know well, for example: Little Red Riding Hood – kind, helpful, polite, caring; the Wolf – sly, cunning, mean, greedy.

Characters

frightened	**rich**
brave	**mean**
cruel	**poor**
terrified	**helpful**
friendly	**nasty**
huge	**clever**

50 LITERACY HOURS FOR LESS ABLE
LEARNERS: Ages 5-7

Character profile

Objectives

Y1. T2. T8.
To identify and discuss characters, for example, appearance, behaviour, qualities; to speculate about how they might behave; to discuss how they are described in the text; and to compare characters from different stories or plays.

Y2. T2. T6.
To identify and describe characters, expressing own views and using words and phrases from texts.

Y2. T2. T14.
To write character profiles, for example, simple descriptions, posters, passports, using key words and phrases that describe or are spoken by characters in the text.

Further support
● If appropriate, let some children make a list of Henry's misdemeanours, using single words and short phrases instead of writing in sentences.

Guided work

1. Before the session fill an old school bag with props including a tatty exercise book, a paper aeroplane, items of school clothing, a catapult or pea shooter and an enlarged copy of the letter from Horrid Henry's teacher from photocopiable page 108, sealed in an envelope.

2. Begin the session by showing the children the bag of props. Reveal the objects one by one. Ask the children to consider what kind of person the items might belong to. Hopefully the children will deduce that they belong to a schoolboy who is not very well behaved.

3. Choose one of the children to take the letter out of the envelope. Display it on the board. Read the text with the children. Clarify the meaning of unfamiliar vocabulary (for example: *sincerely* and *Battle-Axe*). Consider why the boy is called Horrid Henry, who Boudicca Battle-Axe is and why she sent this letter to Henry's parents?

4. Ask the children to describe Horrid Henry's character based on the information given in the text. First, recall some of the awful things he did at school on that day. Then encourage the children to use their imagination and suggest other terrible things Horrid Henry might do at school, for example, in art, PE or on the playground. Use the props introduced at the beginning of the lesson to generate ideas.

5. Pose questions that give the children opportunity to express their own views and opinions about the character, for example: *How would you feel if you had to sit next to Horrid Henry at school? How do you think Horrid Henry's parents felt when they received this letter?*

Independent work
● Explain that Horrid Henry has been in so much trouble this term that he is being sent to a different school. Tell the children that you would like them to pretend they are Horrid Henry's teacher. They must write a short report about him to send to his new school to warn them about his terrible behaviour. Show the children the blank report on the sheet opposite. Ask them to fill in his name and draw a picture in the appropriate spaces and then make general comments about Horrid Henry's terrible behaviour at school and perhaps an overall brief assessment. Before children begin to write, spend a few minutes creating a word bank of key vocabulary on the board.

Plenary
● Hot-seat Horrid Henry. Ask one of the children to take on the role of Horrid Henry. Pretend to be his mum or dad interrogating him about the incidents described in the letter.

School report

Name:

Appearance:

Behaviour:

Comments:

Signed:

Story writing

Objectives
Y1. T1. T9.
To write about events in personal experience linked to a variety of familiar incidents from stories.

Y1. T2. T7.
To discuss reasons for, or causes of, incidents in stories.

Y1. T1–3. T2.
To use phonological, contextual, grammatical and graphic knowledge to work out, predict and check the meanings of unfamiliar words and to make sense of what they read.

Guided work

1. Enlarge a copy of photocopiable page 113. Read the title and ask the children to predict what the story might be about. Read the text and encourage the children to use context cues and their phonic knowledge to work out unfamiliar words. Discuss the story. Ask the children to identify the different characters and describe their behaviour. Highlight how the author creates an image in the readers mind through the use of similes, for example: *they looked like wet washing* and *like two sticky mud cakes.*

2. Underline the sounds made by the cubs as they jump in the mud. Encourage the children to use their phonic knowledge to sound out each of the words. Consider why the author has written these words in capitals. Ask the children to think of words to describe the noises made by the cubs when they splashed in the puddles. Write appropriate suggestions on the board. Encourage the children to tell you the letters you need to write to represent particular sounds.

3. Re-read the story and, this time, allow the children to act out the parts of the naughty bears. Pause at different points and encourage the children to add sound effects and dialogue where appropriate.

4. Copy and cut out the pictures on the sheet opposite. Stick the pictures on the board. Ask the children to describe what the bears are doing in each of the pictures. Work together to sequence the pictures in the order that the incidents occur in the story. Consider why the cubs were able to get up to so much mischief (Father Bear left them on their own while he went out hunting for food in the forest). Ask the children to imagine what Father Bear might have said when he found out about all the naughty things his cubs had done.

5. Ask the children to imagine they have been left home alone. Why have their parents left them by themselves? What naughty things might they do? Ask the children to discuss possible answers to these questions with a partner.

Independent work

● Tell the children that you would like them to turn their ideas into a story. The first part of the story should explain why the children have been left by themselves. The second part should outline two or three naughty things the children do.

Plenary

● Choose different children to read out their stories. Ask the rest of the group to suggest suitable titles or endings.

Further support
● Ask the children to draw a picture to represent each part of the story and then write a simple sentence about each of the pictures.

Story writing

50 LITERACY HOURS FOR LESS ABLE
LEARNERS: Ages 5-7

Setting

Objectives

Y2. T2. T5.

To discuss story settings:
to compare differences; to
locate key words and
phrases in text; to consider
how different settings
influence events and
behaviour.

Y2. T2. T13.

To use story settings from
reading, for example, re-
describe, use in own
writing, write a different
story in the same setting.

Guided Work

1. Before the lesson select a piece of classical music to play to the children. The music you choose should fit the mood of the story setting pictured on photocopiable page 114, for example: '*Lieder Ohne Worte*' OP. 67, No 6 in C Minor by Mendelssohn or '*Gymnopédie No 1*' by Satie. You will also need a toy or cardboard microphone.

2. Enlarge the picture and text on photocopiable page 114 and show it to the group. Explain that it is a page from the beginning of a story book called *Little Polar Bear*. Tell the children that the picture illustrates the *setting* for the beginning of the story. Say that the *setting* is the part of the story that describes where it is going to take place. Ask the children to describe the picture in as much detail as they can and to suggest where it could be.

3. Read the text to the children. Discuss how Lars might feel, drifting alone in the middle of the sea on a piece of ice which is getting smaller and smaller. Ask the children to imagine they are Lars. If you can, dim the lights and then play the music to the group. Encourage the children to crouch down on the floor and pretend they are floating on the small piece of ice in the middle of the sea.

4. Tell the children that you are going to play the music a second time, but this time you will be asking them speak into your magic microphone. Explain that if you hold the microphone in front of them during the music they must say something in character about the story setting. This could be simply a word or phrase. If the children find this activity difficult, you could pose questions to help them respond appropriately, for example: *What is the weather like? Is the sea rough or calm? Can you hear any sounds?* Ask the children to suggest other descriptive words or phrases. Write them on the board.

Independent work

● Give each child a copy of the sheet opposite. Tell them to imagine they are Lars. Ask them to draw a picture of their surroundings in the box and then select appropriate words and phrases from the board to complete the sentences below the picture.

Plenary

● If you have a copy of the story, *Little Polar Bear* by Hans de Beer (North-South Books), read it to the children. Discuss and compare the two contrasting settings used in the story.
● Alternatively, ask the children to make predictions about the story. Will it be a funny, exciting or scary story? Where do they think Lars will drift to? Who might he meet there?

Further support

● Ask the children to imagine they are Lars. Put them in the hot seat. Pose questions that require them to describe the story setting. Record the children's ideas on a tape recorder.

Setting

◼ Draw a picture of Lars at the North Pole.

◼ Imagine you are Lars. Complete the sentences below.

I can see _____

I can hear _____

I can smell _____

I feel _____

Rhyming poetry

Objectives

Y1. T1. T6.

To recite stories and rhymes with predictable and repeating patterns, extemporising on patterns orally by substituting words and phrases, extending patterns, inventing patterns and playing with rhyme.

Y1. T1. T10.

To use rhymes and patterned stories as models for their own writing.

Further support

● Prepare a set of cards with the character names and a set of alternative sentence endings. Ask the children to match the cards to make rhyming sentences.

● Write out some alternative rhyming sentences, for example: *Mr ____ went to the moon.* Ask the children to fill in the rhyming name to complete the sentence.

Guided work

1. Read the poem on photocopiable page 115 with the group. Spend a few minutes discussing the children's reaction to the poem. Hopefully they will have found it amusing. If necessary, explain the meanings of unfamiliar words to the group, for example, *scowl* and *prune*.

2. Re-read the poem. Ask the children to tell you the names of all the people in the house. Write the names as headings on the board. Starting with *Mr Mop*, ask the group to pick out the word that rhymes with each of the names. Write the words on the board. Encourage them to notice that the pairs of rhyming words come in the same line, rather than at the end of different lines, as is the case in many poems.

3. Focus on one pair of rhyming words. Tell the children to listen carefully as you say the two words and ask them to identify the common sound, for example: *an* in *can* and *Pan*. Ask them to suggest other words which contain the *an* rhyme. List the words under the appropriate heading to create a rhyming string. Repeat for the other pairs of rhyming words.

4. Read the lists of rhyming words with the group. You may wish to draw the children's attention to the fact that, in some cases, different groups of letters have been used to represent the same sound, for example: the *oo* sound in *Spoon* and *prune*.

5. Explain to the children that you would like them to help you write some alternative lines for the poem. Model how to pick a word from one of the lists and turn it into a new line for poem, for example: *Mr Mop went to the shop. Mr Plate shut the gate.*

Independent work

● Ask the children to work either individually or in pairs to create new lines for the poem. Provide paper and pencils, so that children can record their ideas and draw pictures to illustrate them. More able writers may be able to write several sentences.

● You may find it necessary to provide some children with the simple writing frame on the sheet opposite. Ask the children to choose a suitable word from the word lists on the board or the word bank at the bottom of the sheet to complete each of the sentences.

Plenary

● Ask each child to read out the rhymes they have invented. Challenge the rest of the group to listen carefully to each sentence and try to identify pairs of rhyming words.

● Can the children suggest a rhyme for a new person, *Mr Bed*?

Rhyming poetry

◀ Choose rhyming words to complete these sentences.

Mr Mop likes to drink _____ .

Mr Pan is a very old _____ .

Mr Bin pricked his finger with a _____ .

Mr Sheet likes to eat _____ .

Mr Spoon went to the _____ .

Mr Door fell on the _____ .

◀ Make up your own rhyming sentences.

Mr _____ .

Mr _____ .

Mr _____ .

Mr _____ .

Mr _____ .

Mr _____ .

| pop | bed | meat | dog | pin |
| man | floor | leg | moon | |

Nursery rhymes

Objectives

Y1. T1. T4.

To read familiar, simple stories and poems independently, to point while reading and make correspondence between words said and read.

Y1. T1. T10.

To use rhymes and patterned stories as models for their own writing.

Guided work

1. Begin the lesson by asking the children to name as many different nursery rhymes as they can. Then ask the group to recite a few of the rhymes that have been suggested.

2. Tell the children that you would like them to read two well-known nursery rhymes with you. Enlarge and display the alternative version of 'Humpty Dumpty' from photocopiable page 116. Tell the children that you would like everyone to read the rhyme together.

3. Have ready the word wand from the sheet opposite. Explain to the children that you are going to use this special wand to point to the words. Read the rhyme on the wand to the children. Ask a child to come and locate the first word of the rhyme. Explain that you are going to point to the words one at a time and you would like the children to watch carefully and say the words as you point to them.

4. Begin reading. Make sure everyone reads together and, if necessary, stop and begin again. When you reach the last line of the rhyme, the children will probably automatically 'read' the traditional ending. Indicate that it cannot say this as there are only three words and they said five.

5. Read the last line together and encourage the children to sound the words out, if necessary. Discuss the children's reactions. Are they surprised or amused by this alternative ending? Can they say what is the difference between this ending and the traditional ending (this one does not rhyme). Ask the children to think of other alternative endings to the rhyme.

6. If you have spent a long time discussing favourite nursery rhymes and describing the wand, you may wish to move straight into the independent activity at this point. Otherwise read 'Hey Diddle, Diddle' from photocopiable page 116 with the group. You could let one of the children use the word wand to point to the words. Ask all the children to suggest their own unusual endings.

Further support

● Use a tape recorder to record a child reciting the nursery rhymes. Play the tape to the children and ask them to point to each word with their wand as they hear it spoken on the tape. Stop the tape at different points to see who is following the text correctly.
● Encourage the children who have difficulty making one-to-one correspondence between spoken and written words to use their word wand during guided or individual reading.

Independent work

● Let all the children cut out their own word wand from card copies of the sheet opposite. Give everyone a copy of one of the nursery rhymes with the final line blanked out. Ask the children to read the poem aloud, pointing to each word as they read. Then ask the children to invent and record their own alternative ending to the rhyme.

Plenary

● Learn together the word wand rhyme.

Word wand

■ Photocopy on to card and then cut out.

I am your magic word wand 1, 2, 3.
Follow the words and read with me.
Point me at the first word of the rhyme.
Read the words from left to right, one at a time.

Action rhymes

Objectives

Y1. T2. T11.
To learn and recite simple poems and rhymes, with actions, and to re-read them from the text.

Y1. T2. T13.
To substitute and extend patterns from reading through language play, for example, by using same lines and introducing new words.

Guided work

1. Read the poem on photocopiable page 117. Pause after each verse to teach the simple action which accompanies it. Re-read the poem. Practise each verse until the children are able to join in confidently with the words and actions.

2. Focus on the structure and pattern of the poem. Ask the children to identify the repeated phrase, two-line verses and rhyming words.

3. Copy and cut up the animal picture cards on the sheet opposite and put them in a bag. Alternatively you could fill the bag with a selection of animal toys. Explain that inside the bag are some other animals you might see at the zoo. Ask the children to guess which animals could be inside the bag.

4. Organise the children so that they are sitting in a circle. Ask everyone to join in and say the repeated line from the poem: *Walking round the zoo, what did I see?* as they pass the bag of animals around the circle. Instruct whoever is holding the bag at the end of the line to take out an animal and tell the rest of the group what it is. Help the group come up with a rhyme about the animal in the same style as the poem, for example: *Walking round the zoo, what did I see? A snake that slithered and hissed at me.* Ask the children simple questions to help generate ideas and draw out appropriate and interesting vocabulary: for example: *How do snakes move? What noise do they make?* Write the new verse on the board and ask the children to devise an action to accompany it.

5. Pass the bag of animals around the circle again. Help the children devise an action rhyme for each of the animals in it. Record the children's ideas on the board. Read the completed poem with the group.

Independent work

● Explain that you would like the group to work together to extend the poem. Give each of the children a copy of the sheet opposite and one of the pictures (or toys) from the bag. Ask everyone to write a sentence about the animal they have been given, in the style of the poem and draw a picture and devise an action to accompany their rhyme.

Plenary

● Re-read the original poem and perform the actions. Then let each child read out their sentence and teach the rest of the group the action they have devised to accompany it. Compile the children's ideas into a book. If possible, allow the group to learn and perform the poem, with actions, to the rest of the class.

Further support

● During the lesson, create a word bank of interesting adjectives and verbs suggested by the children.
● Ask the children to think of two things their animal can do and then help them turn these ideas into a sentence.

Action rhymes

🞕 Write about the animal you have been given.

Walking round the zoo, what did I see? _____

_____

**50 LITERACY HOURS FOR LESS ABLE
LEARNERS: Ages 5-7**

Friendship poems

Objectives

Y1. T1-3. S2.
To use awareness of the grammar of a sentence to decipher new or unfamiliar words.

Y1. T3. T9.
To read a variety of poems on similar themes, for example, families, school, food.

Y1. T3. T15.
To use poems or parts of poems as models for own writing, for example, by substituting words or elaborating on the text.

Further support

● Compose the poem as a group, rather than asking the children to work individually.
● Provide the children with a simple writing frame that requires them just to add an adjective to complete each line of the poem.
● Write together a similar poem where the children have to describe an object which they can actually see and touch, for example: *Apples are... Teddies are...*

Guided work

1. Share the poem '*What are Friends Like?*' on photocopiable page 118. Draw the children's attention to the fact that the title of the poem is written like a question. After reading it, discuss how the poem answers the question in the title. Ask the children to listen carefully as you read each verse in turn. Can they identify the rhyming words in the poem?

2. Read the second poem '*What is a Friend?*' on photocopiable page 119. Notice again that the title is a question which is answered by the poem. Briefly discuss the layout and structure of the poem. Ask the children questions which will draw their attention to key structural features of the poem, for example: *How many verses does the poem have? How many lines does each verse have? Can you see which words are the same in every line of the poem? Can you tell me which words in each verse are rhyming words?*

3. Write on the whiteboard: *A friend is _____*. Ask the children to suggest adjectives that could be used to complete the sentence, for example: *kind, fun*. List these adjectives on the board. Encourage the children to contribute their own ideas as well as adjectives derived from the shared texts.

4. If you have time, you might wish to give the children the opportunity to talk about their own experiences of friends and friendship. You could ask each child in turn to name one of their friends and say what makes them a good friend.

Independent work

● Tell the children that you would like them to write a simple poem that answers the question, *What is a friend?* Demonstrate on the board how to start each line with the words: *A friend is___*. Explain to the children that you would like them to select a different word from the adjective list on the board or the word bank on the sheet opposite to complete each line of the poem. Reassure the group that, although the poem is similar in structure to the shared text, their poem need not rhyme.

Plenary

● Allow each child to read their poem to the group. If a child has written a rhyming poem, ask the other children to identify the rhyming words.
● Re-read the shared texts together. Split the children into three groups. Give each group a verse of 'What is a Friend?' to learn to recite from memory. Perform the poem with each group reciting the verse they have learned.

What is a friend?

■ Choose from these words to write a friendship poem.

A friend is _____

_____

_____

_____

_____

_____

_____

_____

kind	loyal	fair	fun
cool	terrific	funny	helpful
nice	caring	wonderful	

Alliteration

Guided work

1. Read the title and first line of '*In My Garden*' on photocopiable page 120. Ask the children to predict what kinds of things they think the poem will be about. Read the poem with the children. Identify and discuss the meaning of any unfamiliar vocabulary.

2. Ask some simple questions about the poem, for example: *How many bees were in the garden? What did the writer see seven of in the garden? Which line of the poem do you like best? Why?*

3. Ask the children to consider the layout and structure of the poem, including:

> - the number at the start of every line
> - the repeated pattern of four-word lines
> - the alliterative pattern of the poem.

4. Cover up one of the verbs and ask the children to think of alternatives. Remind them that, to maintain the alliterative pattern, the words they suggest should begin with the same letter as the one to be replaced. Repeat this process with other verbs. Re-read the poem.

5. Tell the children that you would like them to help you write a different poem using the structure of the shared text. Write the title and first line of the poem on the board.

> At the seaside [this is title]
> *Today at the seaside I saw…*

6. Write the next line of the poem with the whole group. Simplify the structure of the poem to a number, noun and verb. Ask the children to think of something you might see at the seaside, for example: *One boat*. Then ask the children to think of a word which begins with *b* to describe what it is doing. Choose one of the words to complete the first line of the poem, for example: *One boat bobbing*.

Independent work

- Ask the children, either individually or in pairs, to think of additional lines for the poem. Give each child a copy of the sheet opposite to record their ideas on.

Plenary

- Working with the whole group, ask the children to feedback their ideas to create a group poem. Read the completed poem together.
- Ask individual children to read out their favourite line to the rest of the group.

Objectives

Y1. T2. T13.
To substitute and extend patterns from reading through language play, for example, by using same lines and introducing new words, extending rhyming or alliterative patterns.

Y2. T1. T7.
To learn, re-read and recite favourite poems, taking account of punctuation; to comment on aspects such as word combinations, sound patterns (such as rhymes, rhythms, alliterative patterns) and forms of presentation.

Y2. T1. T12.
To use simple poetry structures and to substitute own ideas, write new lines.

Further support

- Prepare a simple seaside poem based on this structure. Cover all the adjectives or verbs. Ask the children to predict the concealed words.

At the seaside

■ Use this space to record your ideas. Then complete the poem.

Today at the seaside I saw

one _____   _____

two _____   _____

three _____   _____

four _____   _____

five _____   _____

50 LITERACY HOURS FOR LESS ABLE
LEARNERS: Ages 5–7

Fiction and non-fiction

Objective
Y1. T2. T17.
To use terms 'fiction' and 'non-fiction', noting some of their differing features, for example, layout, titles, contents page, use of pictures, labelled diagrams.

Guided work

1. Put a selection of fiction and non-fiction picture books on display in front of the group. Select the books to ensure they illustrate some of the key features of non-fiction texts, including contents pages, headings, photographs, illustrations, captions and labelled diagrams.

2. Discuss on a simple level the difference between the two types of text. Some are story books and the others are books which give us information. Explain that the story books are called fiction books and the books which give us information are called non-fiction. Tell the children that you would like them to sort the books on display into two piles, according to whether they are fiction or non-fiction texts. Encourage them to give a reason for their decision, for example: *My book has a contents page.*

3. Enlarge the text on the photocopiable sheet on page 121 and read it with the group. Encourage the children to predict and check the meanings of unfamiliar words using phonological and picture cues. Ask the children whether they think this extract has come from a fiction or non-fiction book and why they think this. Can they guess the title of the book (*Birds*)?

4. Discuss the layout and presentation of the text. Highlight the following points: Heading; Labels; Photograph; Caption and Main text.

Independent work

● Copy and cut up the set of word cards on the sheet opposite. Organise the group to work either individually or in pairs. Explain that you would like the children to be *non-fiction detectives* and hunt through the books on display to locate examples of the presentational features you highlighted in the text on photocopiable page 121. First, choose a child to select one of the word cards, reveal it to the rest of the group and point to that feature on the shared text. Then challenge everyone to look through the books on display to find examples of that particular feature. Motivate the children by awarding them a point each time they locate a suitable example. Repeat the activity until all the cards have been selected at least once. Add up the points to find out who is the best non-fiction detective!

Plenary

● Display the word cards on the board. Share a non-fiction book with the group. Point to a particular feature, for example, a caption. Ask a child to come and choose the card which names the feature you have highlighted. Repeat for different features.

Further support
● You may wish to focus on one particular feature of non-fiction texts, for example: ask everyone to find different examples of captions in the books.

Non-fiction

heading

contents page

illustration

caption

photograph

label

Contents page

Objectives
Y1. T2. T18.
To read non-fiction books and understand that the reader doesn't need to go from start to finish but selects according to what is needed.

Y1. T2. T21.
To understand the purpose of contents pages and indexes and to begin to locate information by page numbers and words by initial letter.

Guided work

1. Display a selection of non-fiction books with contents pages. At the beginning of the session, allow the children to choose a book and spend a few minutes looking through it.

2. Show the group a non-fiction book on a theme in which you know they are interested. Ask the children to suggest something they would like to find out about on that subject. Turn over the pages one at a time, searching for information on the suggested topic. After a short while, ask if anyone can suggest a quicker way of finding the information (for example, by using a contents page or index). Model how to use the contents page.

3. Ask the children to locate the contents page in their book. Explain that it is situated at the beginning of a book to enable the reader to locate the specific sections of the text they want to read.

4. Enlarge a copy of photocopiable page 122. Share the words and page numbers. Ask the children to tell you what the book is about and suggest a suitable title. Describe how the book is divided into three main chapters and each of these chapters is divided into smaller subsections. Pose some simple questions for example: *What type of transport can you read about on page 6?*

5. Explain that contents are listed in the order they occur so the numbers on the right of the page are in numerical order. The number alongside each heading indicates the page each new section starts on. Some numbers are missing from the list because a section often extends over more than one page.

Independent work

● Tell the children that you would like them to make a simple picture book with a contents page. Give each child a copy of the sheet opposite. Instruct them to cut the pictures out and clip them together with a paper clip in any order they like. Ask the children to number the pages in order, one to five, and then fill in the contents page.
● Children who finish quickly could also make a front cover or an additional page for their book.

Plenary

● Tell the children to swap books amongst themselves. Ask questions, for example: *Which page would you turn to if you wanted to look at a picture of a boat? What picture would you see if you turned to page 5 in your book?* Encourage the children to use the contents page to answer the questions.

Further support
● Cut up and reassemble the photocopiable sheet on page 124 to stress that sections are listed in numerical order.
● If you have multiple copies of a simple non-fiction text, challenge the children to use the contents page to race to locate specific sections in the book.

Contents page

■ Make this little book on transport. Then write the contents page.

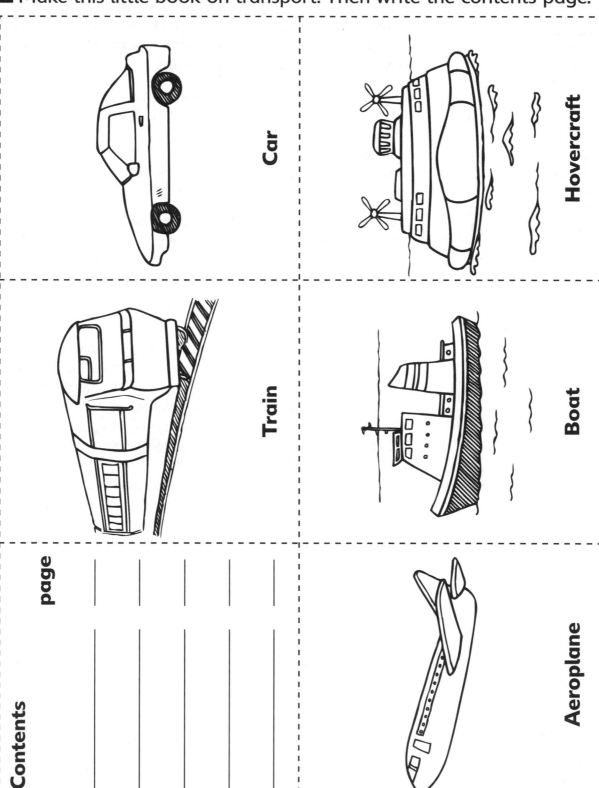

50 LITERACY HOURS FOR LESS ABLE
LEARNERS: Ages 5-7

Non-chronological reports

Objectives

Y1. T2. T17.
To use terms 'fiction' and 'non-fiction', noting some of their differing features, for example, layout, titles, contents page, use of pictures, labelled diagrams.

Y1. T2. T25.
To use simple sentences to describe, based on examples from reading; to write simple non-chronological reports; and to organise in lists, separate pages, charts.

Guided work

1. Show the group a copy of photocopiable page 121. If you have taught 'Fiction and non-fiction' on page 86, the children will already be familiar with this text. Begin the lesson by simply re-reading and recapping the main points of the passage.

2. If the text is new to the group, begin the session by explaining that it is an extract from a non-fiction book called *Birds.* Read the text with the group. Highlight specific presentational features, including the heading, photograph, labels, bullet points and caption. Pose simple questions which require the children to recall facts from the text, for example: *What do all birds have in common? Which bird cannot fly?*

3. Explain to the children that this non-fiction text is an example of a non-chronological report. Describe in very simple terms some of the organisational features of non-chronological reports which are illustrated by this text extract.

- Facts are organised in non-chronological order.
- It is written in the present tense.
- A general introductory classification is given, followed by a more detailed description of particular characteristics. (Ask the children to suggest other information which they think may be contained in subsequent pages of this book about birds.)
- The text begins by describing birds generally (*All birds...*), and then moves to give more specific examples (*Most birds...*).

4. Share the text 'Making a nest' on photocopiable page 123. If possible, have a nest to show the children. Discuss why birds make nests. Ask the children to recall and describe how different birds construct their nests. Draw simple pictures on the board to help children visualise and remember the different types of nests.

Independent work

- Each child will need a copy of the sheet opposite, scissors, a sheet of A3 plain paper and writing equipment. Explain that you would like everyone to make their own page of non-fiction writing about how birds make their nests. Ask the children to cut up the sentence openings and endings and then match them up correctly. They should then copy or glue the sentences they have made on to a sheet of A3 paper and add a heading and appropriate illustrations.

Plenary

- Ask one of the children to show their work. Let the group think of suitable captions to go with the pictures they have drawn.

Further support

- You may find it useful to spread this lesson over two sessions, so that you can spend longer discussing with the children how they are going to set out their work.
- Read other books about birds and discuss the sort of information they contain and how this information is organised and presented.

Making a nest

Read these broken sentences, then put them back together.

Most birds

Some birds

Woodpeckers

A nest

peck holes in trees to make their nests.

dig holes in the earth to make a nest.

keeps a bird's eggs safe and warm.

build nests with grass, twigs and mud.

50 LITERACY HOURS FOR LESS ABLE
LEARNERS: Ages 5-7

Explanation

Objectives
Y1. T2. T22.
To write labels for drawings and diagrams.

Y2. T1-3. T2.
To use phonological, contextual, grammatical and graphic knowledge to work out, predict and check the meanings of unfamiliar words and to make sense of what they read.

Y2. T2. T19.
To read flow charts and cyclical diagrams that explain a process.

Y2. T2. T21.
To produce simple flow charts or diagrams that explain a process.

Guided work

1. Show the group the text on photocopiable page 124. Tell the children that the extract is taken from a non-fiction book called *Tadpoles and Frogs.* Read the words with the children. Encourage them to predict and check the meanings of unfamiliar words using phonological, picture and context cues.

2. Discuss the information presented in the extract. Explain that the text describes how a tadpole develops into a frog. Ask the children to spend a few minutes discussing with a partner the way in which a tadpole changes as it grows up and turns into a frog, based on what they have learned from the passage.

3. Spend a few moments considering the structural features of this non-fiction text. Ask the children to explain why 'Growing up' is written in larger print? Notice that the different stages of the life cycle are numbered. Do the children think the pictures help to explain the process more clearly?

4. Prepare enlarged copies of the pictures and text on the sheet opposite. Stick the pictures on the board and ask the children to help you sequence them correctly. Number the pictures and draw arrows between them to make it clear to the children that the stages of development from tadpole to frog always occur in the same order. Give everyone in the group one of the captions to read and match to the correct picture.

5. Write the heading *Growing up* above the diagram. Use bold letters to reiterate the idea that the heading needs to stand out on the page.

Independent work

● Give each child a copy of the pictures on the sheet opposite. Instruct the children to sequence the pictures in the correct order and then stick them down. Ask them to number the pictures from one to five and then write a simple caption to go with each one.

Plenary

● Rearrange the pictures on the board to form a cyclical diagram. Ask the children to tell you what happens after the tadpole has become a frog (it lays eggs called frogspawn and then a tadpole hatches out from each of the eggs). Draw pictures to represent these stages on the board. Ask the children to suggest a suitable caption for each picture. Introduce the idea that the diagram shows the life cycle of a frog. Reiterate that the stages always occur in the same order and that the cycle is continuous.

Further support
● Provide the children with simple captions to match to the pictures.

From tadpole to frog

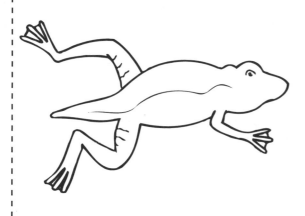

50 LITERACY HOURS FOR LESS ABLE
LEARNERS: Ages 5-7

Captions

Objectives

Y1. T1. S8.
To begin using full stops to demarcate sentences.

Y1. T1. T14.
To write captions for their own work.

Guided work

1. Show the group a photograph of themselves or other children in the class taking part in a routine school activity. Ask simple questions to encourage descriptions of what is happening in the photograph: *Who is in the picture? What are they doing?* Give each member of the group a photograph of children engaged in a different activity. Ask them to look carefully at the picture and then describe it in as much detail as they can to the rest of the group.

2. Tell the group that they are to make a booklet of photographs to show new parents the kinds of activities which their children would do if they attended your school. Ask the children to consider how parents looking at the booklet would know what the children are doing in the photographs. Elicit the need for some kind of label or caption for each picture to explain what activity it shows.

3. Select one of the photographs. Discuss what is happening in the picture. Ask pairs of children to think together of a sentence which they could write to describe what the photograph shows. Let each pair of children say their sentence to the rest of the group. Choose one of the sentences and model writing it on the board. Emphasise the use of a capital letter at the start of the sentence and a full stop at the end. Read the sentence together and see if it performs its function well. Repeat with the other sentences suggested by the children.

Independent work

● Give each child a copy of the sheet opposite and let them choose one of the photographs. Explain that, before they stick the photographs down, you would like everyone to write a caption to go with the photograph they have chosen. The caption should be written neatly on the lines below the box. Remind the children to use proper punctuation, for example: starting their sentence with a capital letter.

Plenary

● When everyone has completed their caption, tell the children that you are going to find out how good the captions are. Mix up the photographs in the middle of the table. Choose a child to read one of the captions out. Encourage the other children to look for the photograph which best fits the caption. Repeat until all the photographs and captions are matched correctly.

● Finish by sticking each photograph in the correct picture box and adding a front cover to the album. Challenge the group to devise a suitable title.

Further support
● The children could complete this activity with a partner.
● Allowing the children to word-process their captions may help to engage more reluctant writers.
● Display captioned pictures, such as those on the photocopiable sheets on pages 121 and 123.

Captions

◼ Choose a photograph and stick it in this space. Write a caption for it.

50 LITERACY HOURS FOR LESS ABLE
LEARNERS: Ages 5-7

Labels

Objective
Y1. T2. T22.
To write labels for drawings and diagrams, for example, growing beans, parts of the body.

Guided work

1. Copy and enlarge the diagrams on the sheet opposite on to two separate sheets of paper. Display the first picture. Cover the explanatory sentence and the labels with strips of paper that can be easily peeled off by the children to reveal the words underneath.

2. Tell the children the picture was sent to you by an alien. Begin by asking the children to tell you what they think it is a picture of. Encourage everyone to guess, however silly their ideas may sound.

3. Explain that it is actually a drawing of the alien's *computer.* Reveal and read out the sentence at the top of the page. Establish that, although the computer looks very different from the ones the children use at school, the sentence informs us that the names of the parts of the computer are the same, for example: *mouse* and *printer.* Ask the children to try and guess which part of the alien computer is which. Choose different children to reveal and read the labels.

4. Reiterate the idea that the sentence and the labelled diagram contain the same information. Ask the children to consider whether they found the sentence or the labels most useful when interpreting the picture. Discuss the children's ideas. Encourage them to appreciate the usefulness of the diagram, for example: *It illustrates what the computer looks like and has labels joined to the main features of the computer to show what they are called.*

Independent work

● Display the second picture. Tell the children that you would like them to send the alien a picture of their computer. Explain that the alien will not have seen a computer like this before. Ask the children to consider the following questions: *Do they think the alien will know what it is a picture of? Could they add anything to the picture of the computer to make it more informative?*
● Give each child a photocopy of the picture of the computer, or ask them to draw a picture themselves. Ask the children to use the words in the box, and any others they can think of themselves, to label the parts of the computer correctly. Remind them to draw a line joining each label to the correct part of the picture.

Further support
● Label some real objects, for example: a bike, a person or a tree. Then ask the children to complete a labelled drawing of the same object.
● Provide opportunities for the children to draw labelled diagrams to annotate simple instructions - see the lesson 'Instructions 1' on page 98.
● Use the labelled pictures to reinforce learning on nouns.

Plenary

● Show the children a copy of photocopiable page 125. Encourage them to use the picture cues to help them read the words. Discuss the presentation of the labels. Ask the children to say how these labels are similar to those used on the picture of the computer you looked at in the main part of the lesson.

Labels

This is a computer. It has a mouse, a keyboard, a monitor and a printer.

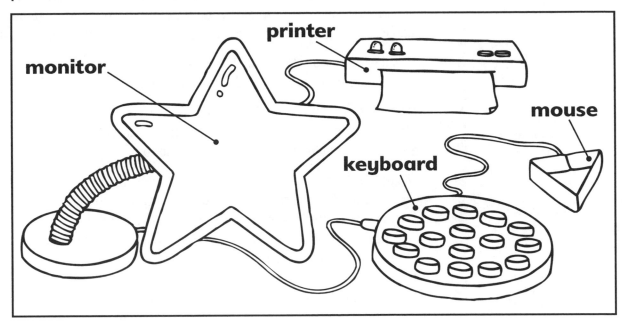

◼ Label this computer.

mouse	**keyboard**	**printer**
headphones	**monitor**	

Instructions 1

Guided work

1. Tell the group that you are going to look at an example of an instruction text. Discuss with the children their own experiences of using instructions, for example: receipes, or instructions for a game. Emphasise the idea that instructions tell people how to do something.

2. Display a copy of photocopiable page 126. Ask the children to locate and read the title to find out what the instructions are for.

3. Read through the text with the group. At a simple level, direct the children's attention to some of the key structural features of this genre which are illustrated by these instructions:

- a clear title
- the use of short, concise sentences written in the imperative
- numbered steps, each step beginning on a new line
- the use of words such as *first, then* and *finally* to emphasise the chronological sequence of the instructions.

4. Invite the children to stand up. Tell them that you would like them to pretend they are following the instructions to make a snowman. Read the instructions out in the wrong order. This is a simple but effective means of giving the children an appreciation of the need to follow instructions in chronological order. The children will quickly realise that, because each instruction builds on the preceding one, it is vital to sequence them correctly. They would find it very difficult to put on the snowman's hat if they had not first made his head!

5. Ask the children to consider whether they think the instructions are easy to follow. Do they think someone who has never made a snowman before could follow these instructions? Encourage the children to try and think of a way they could be improved for someone who does not know what a snowman is. Introduce the idea of using pictures or diagrams to illustrate each step.

Independent work

- Give all the children a set of the instructions on the sheet opposite. Direct the children to follow the instructions to make a snowman out of Plasticine. Ask them to draw a picture in each box to illustrate what the snowman looks like after each instruction.

Plenary

- Look at the children's instruction sheets. Discuss how the instructions have been improved by the addition of illustrations to clarify the written text.

How to make a snowman

First roll a big ball of snow.	Next roll a smaller ball of snow.
Put the small snowball on top of the big snowball.	Stick the twigs into the big snowball to make the snowman's arms.
Put a carrot in the middle of the small snowball for the snowman's nose.	Then use two stones to make the snowman's eyes.
Use some more stones to make the snowman's mouth.	Finally, dress your snowman in a scarf and hat to keep him warm!

Instructions 2

Objectives

Y1. T1. T13.
To read and follow simple instructions.

Y2. T1. T13.
To read simple written instructions.

Y2. T1. T15.
To write simple instructions.

Y2. T1. T18.
To use appropriate register in writing instructions, that is, direct, impersonal, building on texts read.

Guided work

1. Play a quick game of 'What am I doing?' Tell all of the children except one to stand with their backs to you. Perform a simple action, for example: put your hands on your head. The child who is 'it' must watch what you do and then direct the rest of the group to do the same. Let the children take turns to be 'it' and encourage them to be as bossy as possible when giving instructions!

2. Show the group an enlarged copy of the treasure map on the sheet opposite. Allow the children a few minutes to look at the pictures on the map and read the labels. Tell the group that this map once belonged to a pirate who buried some treasure on the island. He drew this map so that he or one of his fellow pirates would be able to retrieve the treasure years later.

3. Show the children the written directions on photocopiable page 127. Read the heading *Directions to the treasure*. Explain that you are going to read and follow the written directions together to try to locate the place where the pirate buried his treasure.

4. Read the first instruction together. Ask one of the group to Blu-Tack a counter on the map in the correct start position. Read each of the instructions in turn. After each direction, choose a different child to move the counter to mark the location reached. Repeatedly draw the children's attention to the direct, impersonal way in which the directions are given. Ask the children to consider why instructions are written in this way.

Independent work

● Organise the children in pairs sitting with a screen between them. Give each child a copy of the sheet opposite and a counter. Tell one child in each pair that they are the pirate and must draw a cross on their map where they have buried their treasure. The 'pirate' must then give instructions to their partner to help them locate the place where the treasure is buried. Spend some time working alongside each pair, praising the use of concise, 'bossy' directions.
● Ask the children to work together in their pairs to write the oral exercise as a set of simple numbered instructions. You may wish to model this first. You will find this a lot to fit into one lesson and may wish to carry the written activity over to a subsequent literacy session with the group.

Further support

● Choose children to lead a game of 'Simon says'.
● Practise shared writing of simple directions, for example: how to get from the classroom to the hall.

Plenary

● Let one child read out their written instructions. The rest of the group should try to follow the directions to locate the treasure.

Treasure island

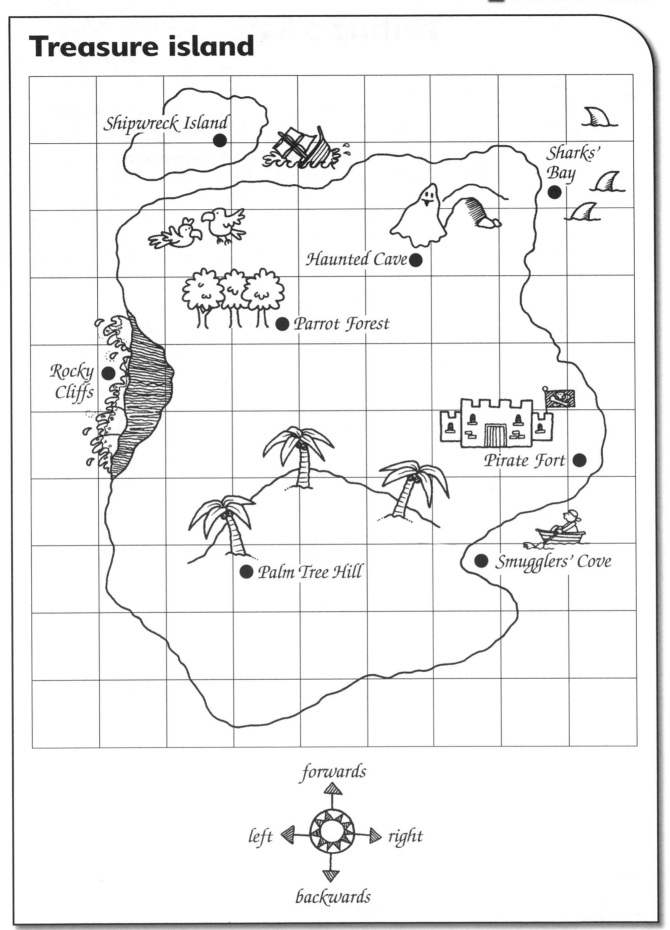

Writing a list

Objectives
Y1. T1. T15.
To make simple lists for planning, reminding, etc.

Guided work

1. In preparation for this lesson you will need to obtain a teddy bear and a holiday brochure advertising holidays in a sunny destination.

2. Introduce Teddy to the group. Tell the children that Teddy is very excited because he is going on holiday tomorrow. Show the group a picture of the hotel Teddy is going to stay in. Ask if any of the children have ever been to Spain. Let the children who have, tell Teddy a bit about what it is like and the type of activities you can do there. Make sure you draw the children's attention to the fact that the weather in Spain is generally sunny and hot.

3. Explain to the children that Teddy has never visited a hot country before. He is worried because he does not really know what sort of things he will need to pack in his suitcase. Suggest to the children that they could help Teddy with his problem.

4. Ask the children to sit in a circle. Pass Teddy around the circle, allowing each child to recommend one or two things they think he should pack in his suitcase, for example: suncream, shorts, sun-hat.

5. Once all the children have had a turn, ask Teddy if that has been helpful to him. Hold Teddy up to your ear to make it look like he is whispering something to you. Tell the children Teddy is worried that he will not be able to remember all the things they have told him to pack when he gets home. Ask them what they could do to help him remember all the items. Hopefully one of the group will suggest writing a list.

6. Choose one of the items suggested by the children and write it on the whiteboard. Say the word aloud as you write it. Demonstrate as you write how to segment the word into sounds. Ask the children to tell you the letters you need to write to represent those sounds.

7. Decide with the group what the second item on the list is going to be. Once again, involve the children in the spelling of the word. Request guidance from the group about the layout of a list, for example: each item should be written under the preceding one.

Independent work

● Give each child a copy of the sheet opposite. Ask them to copy the list of words you have made together and then extend the list with more ideas of their own.

Plenary

● Let each child read out their list and then present it to Teddy.

Further support
● Create other meaningful contexts for writing lists, for example, a shopping list.
● Numbering each of the items in a list may help the children to remember to write each item on a new line.

Holiday list

◀ Help Teddy pack his suitcase. Write a list of what he needs to take.

Recount

Objectives

Y1. T3. T18.
To read recounts and begin to recognise generic structure, for example, ordered sequence of events, use of words like *first, next, after, when*.

Y2. T1. T11.
To use language of time to structure a sequence of events, for example, '*when I had finished...*', '*suddenly...*', '*after that...*'.

Guided work

1. Before the session gather together a pillow, towel, jumper, cereal box or orange-juice carton, toothbrush or toothpaste, shoes and a coat. Make a word card for each of the time connectives highlighted in bold on photocopiable page 128.

2. Discuss with the children how they get ready for school in the morning. Pose questions to encourage the children to consider the order in which they perform different tasks.

3. Read the text on photocopiable page 128 with the children. Discuss Sam's morning ritual and how it is similar or different to the routines described by the children in the group. Draw the children's attention to the time connectives written in bold text.

4. Tell the group that you would like them to work together to recount how Sam gets ready for school. Display the props in front of the group. Give each child in the group a word card. Ask the children to stand in a line in the order the words appear in the text. Next re-read the text and pause at appropriate points to allow the children to collect the prop which matches their time word. The first child might begin by pretending to lift their head from the pillow, stretching and then saying: *At seven o'clock Sam got out of bed.* Continue along the line until the recount is complete. Ensure all of the children say their time word somewhere in their sentence.

5. Ask the children if they think it would matter if the time words were arranged in a different order. Discuss the meaning of the words *first* and *finally*. Stress that these words only make sense in a particular place. Swap some of the other time words around to show that they can be used with greater flexibility. Redistribute the time words among the children and ask them to stand in a different place. Repeat the oral activity.

Independent work

● Give each child a copy of the pictures on the sheet opposite. Tell them to cut out and sequence the pictures in order and write a sentence which includes a time word on a separate piece of paper. Alternatively, you could enlarge the pictures and make a group book. Give each child one picture and ask them to write about it.

Plenary

● Chose a child to give an oral recount of how they get ready for school. The rest of the group should listen and give a thumbs up for every time connective they hear.

Further support

● Ask the children to write simple recounts of school visits.
● Highlight time connectives in shared reading. Make a word bank of these words.

Getting ready

50 LITERACY HOURS FOR LESS ABLE
LEARNERS: Ages 5-7

Dictionary work

Objectives

Y1. T1. W2.
To practise and secure alphabetic letter knowledge and alphabetic order.

Y2. T2. T16.
To use dictionaries and glossaries to locate words by using initial letter.

Y2. T2. T17.
To learn that dictionaries and glossaries give definitions and explanations; discuss what definitions are, explore some simple definitions in dictionaries.

Y2. T2. T20.
To make class dictionaries and glossaries of special interest words, giving explanations and definitions, for example, linked to topics.

Further support

● Let the children make other pages for the dictionary. They could write their own simple definitions.
● Give the group lots of opportunities to look up different words in simple dictionaries, glossaries and other alphabetically ordered texts.

Guided work

1. In preparation for this activity you will need to enlarge and cut out a set of the letters, labels and definitions on the sheet opposite and alphabet strips from page 57. Tell the children that you would like them to help you make a picture dictionary. The example given here is for a simple animal dictionary, but ideally you should make a dictionary giving explanations of words linked to your class topic work.

2. Put a selection of simple picture dictionaries on display in front of the group. Discuss with the children on a simple level what the purpose of a dictionary is, for example: *to explain what words mean.*

3. Ask the group if anyone can describe how the text in a dictionary is organised. If necessary, remind the children that the words in a dictionary are arranged in the same order as the letters of the alphabet. Explain how this makes it easier to find a word you want to look up the meaning of.

4. Reiterate that the letters of the alphabet always come in the same order. Hand out an alphabet strip to each child. Sing or chant the letters of the alphabet in order. Encourage the children to point to each letter on their alphabet strip as they say its name.

5. Let each child select a dictionary and spend a few minutes looking at it independently. Play the 'Word race' game to test the children's knowledge of alphabetical order. Write a letter on the board. Challenge the children to be the first to find a word in their dictionary beginning with that letter. Let the winner read out the word they have found and its definition. Repeat for different letters.

Independent work

● Ask the children to sit in a circle. Spread the letter cards out face down. Let each child choose a letter card in turn. Now spread out the word cards in front of the group. Ask each child to take the word which begins with their letter and read it out to the rest of the group. Finally display one of the definitions. Read it with the children and ask who thinks the definition matches their word. Repeat until everyone has collected a definition applicable to their word.
● Show the children how to make a page for the dictionary. Instruct them to either copy out or stick the animal name and definition on to a sheet of A4 paper and then draw a picture of the animal.

Plenary

● Ask each child to show their completed page. Help the children order the pages alphabetically. Read the dictionary together.

Animal dictionary

d e h z k r g t	
dog	Four-legged animal that barks. Many people keep it as a pet.
elephant	The largest living land animal. It is grey and has a long trunk.
horse	A hoofed animal which is used for riding and to pull loads.
zebra	A horse-like animal with black and white stripes.
kangaroo	An animal which travels by jumping. It carries its young in a pouch.
rabbit	A small animal with long ears and a fluffy tail.
giraffe	The tallest living animal. It has four legs and a very long neck. Its coat has lots of dark patches.
tiger	A fierce meat-eating big cat. It has an orange coat with black stripes.

50 LITERACY HOURS FOR LESS ABLE
LEARNERS: Ages 5-7

Horrid Henry Gets Rich Quick

Dear Henry's Parents,
I am sorry to tell you that
today Henry:
Poked William
Tripped Linda
Shoved Dave
Pinched Andrew
Made rude noises, chewed gum,
and would not stop talking in class
Yours Sincerely
            Boudicca Battle-Axe

Henry scowled.

"Can I help it if I have to burp?"

"And what about all the children you hurt?" said Dad.

"I hardly touched William. Linda got in my way, and Dave and Andrew annoyed me," said Henry. What a big fuss over nothing.

"Right," said Dad. "I am very disappointed with you. No TV, no comics and no sweets for a week."

"A WEEK!" screamed Henry. "For giving someone a little tap? It's not fair!"

Francesca Simon

Bedtime

"Bedtime in **five** minutes!
Put away your toys."
"But I don't want to go to bed."

"Bedtime in **four** minutes!
Go and wash your face."
"But I don't want to go to bed."

"Bedtime in **three** minutes!
Come and have your milk."
"But I don't want to go to bed."

"Bedtime in **two** minutes!
Go and brush your teeth."
"But I don't want to go to bed."

"Bedtime in **one** minute!
Let me tuck you in."
"But I don't want to go to bed!"

"BEDTIME NOW!"

Louise Carruthers

The Little Red Hen

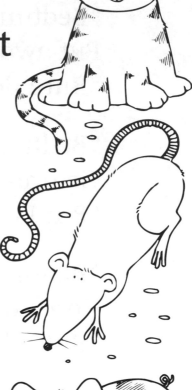

"Who will help me plant this wheat?"

"Not I," said the cat.

"Not I," said the rat.

"Not I," said the pig.

"Then I will do it myself!" said the Little Red Hen.

50 LITERACY HOURS FOR LESS ABLE
LEARNERS: Ages 5-7

SCHOLASTIC

The Minpins

Little billy's mother was always telling him exactly what he was allowed to do and what he was not allowed to do.

All the things he was allowed to do were boring. All the things he was not allowed to do were exciting.

One of the things he was NEVER NEVER allowed to do, the most exciting of them all, was to go out through the garden gate all by himself and explore the world beyond.

Roald Dahl

Goldilocks
and the Three Bears

The three bears came back from their walk. The father bear looked at the table and then he said in his deep, gruff voice,

"WHO'S BEEN EATING MY PORRIDGE?"

The mother bear looked and she said in her soft, low voice,

"WHO'S BEEN EATING MY PORRIDGE?"

And last of all the little bear saw his bowl and he cried out in his shrill, high voice,

"WHO'S BEEN EATING MY PORRIDGE AND EATEN IT ALL UP?"

Retold by Penelope Lively

Father Bear and the Naughty Bear Cubs

Once upon a time there was a Father Bear who lived in a cave with his two little bear cubs.

Every day Father Bear had to go into the forest to hunt for food, and every day, while he was away, the little bears were naughty. They splashed in puddles until they looked like wet washing. They wandered off and got lost. They growled and they quarrelled.

One day, when their father had gone hunting, the two little bears went for a walk in the forest. By and by, they came to a muddy patch, and – guess what they did. They jumped SPLOSH! straight into the mud and stomped about SQUISHY-SQUASHY! SQUELCH! SQUELCH! until they looked like two sticky mud cakes.

Margaret Mayo

Little Polar Bear

When Lars woke up it was morning. He was alone in the middle of the sea. It was getting warmer and warmer and the piece of ice and Lars's pile of snow were getting smaller and smaller.

Hans de Beer

People in the house

Mr Mop has a floppy top.
Mr Broom wants a bit more room.

Mr Brush is in a rush.
Mr Pan goes as quick as he can.

Mr Plate is very late.
Mr Cup is getting up.

Mr Spoon is eating a prune.
Mr Bin is giving a grin.

Mr Towel is making a scowl.
Mr Sheet has got smelly feet.

Charles Thomson

Nursery crimes

Humpty Dumpty Sat on the Wall

Humpty Dumpty sat on the wall,

Humpty Dumpty had a great fall.

All the King's horses and all the King's men

trod on him.

Hey Diddle, Diddle

Hey diddle, diddle,

the cat and the fiddle,

the cow jumped over the moon.

The little dog laughed

to see such fun,

and the dish ran away with the chocolate biscuits.

Michael Rosen

Walking Round the Zoo

Walking round the zoo,
What did I see?

An elephant that waved
Its trunk at me.

Walking round the zoo,
What did I see?

A parrot that squawked
And winked at me.

Walking round the zoo,
What did I see?

A crocodile that snapped
Its jaws at me.

Walking round the zoo,
What did I see?

A monkey that pointed
And laughed at me!

John Foster

50 LITERACY HOURS FOR LESS ABLE
LEARNERS: Ages 5-7

What are friends like?

Friends are kind,
Friends are fun,
Friends can talk and listen too,
Friends can help,
Friends can hug,
You like them and they like you.

Friends can share,
Friends can care,
Friends can play with you all day,
Friends can say sorry
Friends forgive,
Friends don't sulk or run away.

Friends are good,
Friends are great,
Friends can laugh and joke with you,
Friends are true,
Friends are fond,
Friends enjoy the things you do.

I like friends, don't you?

Ruth Kirtley

What is a friend?

A friend is kind.
A friend is fair.
A friend will always let you share.

A friend is faithful.
A friend is true.
A friend will always stick by you.

A friend is fun.
A friend is great.
A friend will always be your mate!

Louise Carruthers

**50 LITERACY HOURS FOR LESS ABLE
LEARNERS: Ages 5-7**

In my garden

In my garden I can see
One tall tree towering
Two small squirrels scampering
Three beautiful butterflies bowing
Four dainty daisies dancing
Five lovely ladybirds lazing
Six crazy caterpillars crawling
Seven wiggly worms waving
Eight slow snails sliding
Nine sunny sunflowers smiling
Ten busy bees buzzing

Louise Carruthers

What is a bird?

All birds:

- have two wings
- have feathers
- have a **beak**
- **lay** eggs

Most birds:

- can fly
- make a nest to lay their eggs in.

feathers

wing

beak

Penguins are birds that cannot fly. They use their wings to help them swim.

Rod Theodorou

50 LITERACY HOURS FOR LESS ABLE LEARNERS: Ages 5-7

Contents

50 LITERACY HOURS FOR LESS ABLE
LEARNERS: Ages 5-7

■SCHOLASTIC

Photographs © Ingram Publishing and Marathon Oil Co. via Soda

Making a nest

Most birds build nests. They build them with things they can easily find, like grass, twigs and mud. The nest will keep their eggs warm and safe from **enemies**.

This hummingbird nest shows how they build using grass, twigs and mud

Some birds dig holes into the earth to make their nests. Woodpeckers peck holes in trees or **cacti** to live in. Sometimes other birds nest in old woodpecker nests.

Woodpeckers make their nests by pecking holes in trees

Rod Theodorou

Photographs © Corel

Growing up

As a tadpole grows up, it turns into a frog. Follow the numbers to see how.

1. Two legs grow near its tail.

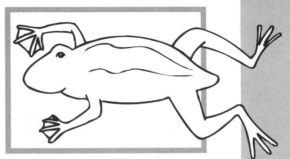

4. Soon its tail has almost gone.

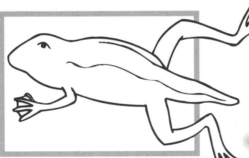

2. Next, two legs grow near the front.

5. Now it has become a frog.

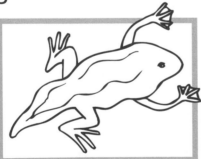

3. Its tail gets shorter.

Anna Milbourne

Number 37

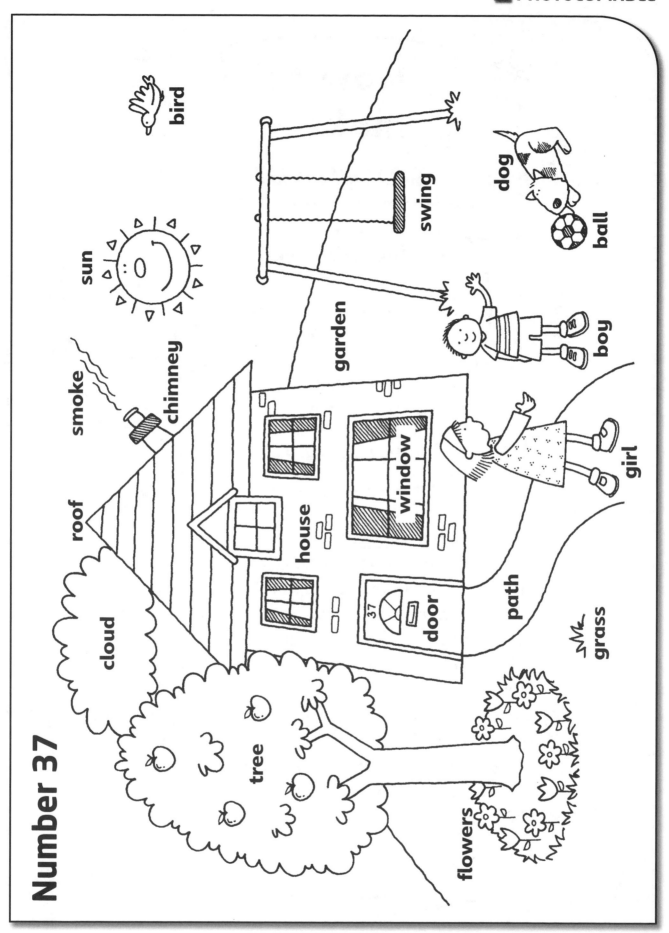

How to make a snowman

You will need

snow
2 sticks or long twigs
a carrot
a scarf
a hat
stones

What to do

1. First roll a big ball of snow.
2. Next roll a smaller ball of snow.
3. Put the small snowball on top of the big snowball.
4. Stick the twigs into the big snowball – one on each side to make the snowman's arms.
5. Push the carrot in the middle of the small snowball to make a nose.
6. Then use two of the stones to make the snowman's eyes.
7. Make a curved mouth with the rest of the stones. (If you have some left over, put them in a line on the bottom snowball to make coat buttons.)
8. Finally, dress your snowman in a scarf to keep him warm!

50 LITERACY HOURS FOR LESS ABLE LEARNERS: Ages 5-7

SCHOLASTIC

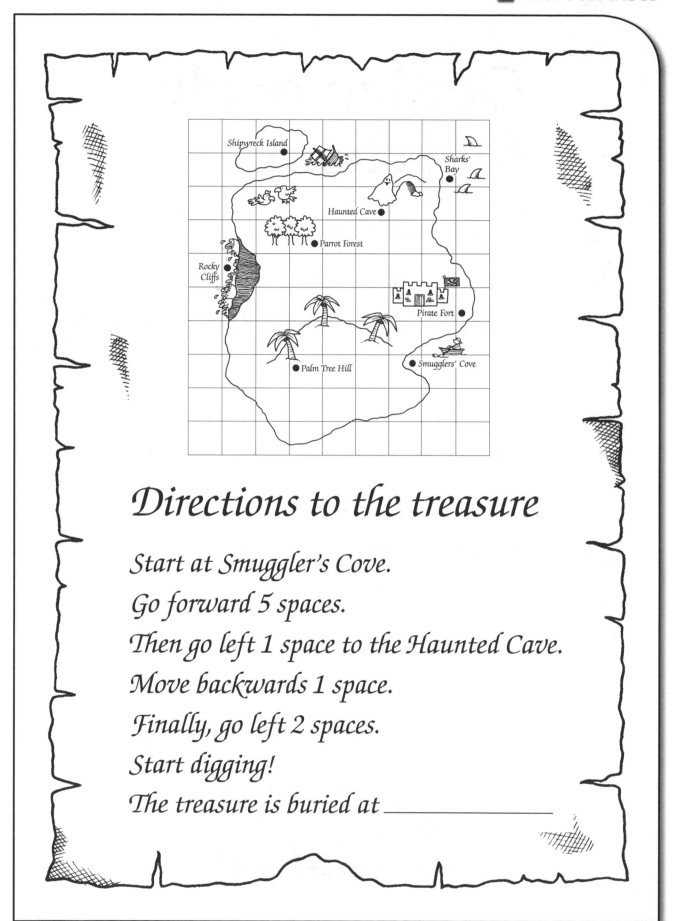

Directions to the treasure

Start at Smuggler's Cove.

Go forward 5 spaces.

Then go left 1 space to the Haunted Cave.

Move backwards 1 space.

Finally, go left 2 spaces.

Start digging!

The treasure is buried at _____

Getting ready for school

At **seven o'clock** Sam got up. **First** he went into the bathroom to wash his face and comb his hair. **Then** he went back to his bedroom to put his school uniform on. **After that** Sam went downstairs to have his breakfast. He had some toast and a drink of orange. **Next** Sam brushed his teeth. **Finally** he put on his shoes and coat and set off to go to school.

50 LITERACY HOURS FOR LESS ABLE
LEARNERS: Ages 5-7